Mona Hamadeh has lived between Lebanon and the UK for many years. She learned to cook traditional Lebanese food from her mother and grandmother in Lebanon, observing them from the age of five. Since moving to the UK as a young woman, the passion she felt for Lebanese cuisine has been expressed through the food she prepares for her own children and grandchildren. She believes that Lebanese cuisine represents one of the world's healthiest diets, and that the Lebanese concept of 'sharing bread and salt' as a means of demonstrating friendship and love is a wonderful code for family life.

Mona ran classes in Lebanese cooking in her local area for many years. As an English/Arabic interpreter for various companies and hospitals, she not only provided her language skills but also cooked Lebanese meals as a way of offering a taste of familiarity to those far from home.

A LEBANESE FEAST

OF VEGETABLES, PULSES, HERBS AND SPICES

MONA HAMADEH

A HOW TO BOOK

ROBINSON

ROBINSON

First published in Great Britain in 2015 by Robinson

Copyright © Mona Hamadeh, 2015

3 5 7 9 10 8 6 4

The moral right of the author has been asserted.

A CIP catalogue record for this book
is available from the British Library.

ISBN: 978-1-84528-579-1

Typeset in Great Britain by Ian Hughes, www.mousematdesign.com
Printed and bound in Italy by L.E.G.O. S.p.A.

Robinson
An imprint of
Little, Brown Book Group
Carmelite House
50 Victoria Embankment
London EC4Y 0DZ

An Hachette UK Company
www.hachette.co.uk

www.littlebrown.co.uk

How To Books are published by Robinson, an imprint of Little, Brown Book Group. We welcome proposals from authors who have first-hand experience of their subjects. Please set out the aims of your book, its target market and its suggested contents in an email to Nikki.Read@howtobooks.co.uk

Contents

Author's Notes

Here are a few notes on the way the recipes are presented and some tips on storage and cooking.

- In this type of cooking there are no rules (apart from baking); it often comes down to individual taste and preference.

- The ingredients are listed in the order in which they are used in the recipe.

- The preparation time given is an indication only. It will depend on the individual, as some people work faster than others; using a blunt knife can also mean it takes longer to get the job done.

- Cooking times may also vary slightly, give and take a few minutes, according to oven type. While writing this book I had to use different ovens, depending on where I was living at the time. In Lebanon I use propane gas, which is hotter than the natural gas used in the UK, and sometimes I had to use an ancient electric cooker, which took forever.

- The number of servings given is mostly on the generous side. When I say serves four, the recipe may actually feed six. If you have guests with a good appetite, these portions save the embarrassment of not having enough.

- I have offered ideas for serving suggestions throughout.

- You will find useful basic recipes in the last chapter. These are frequently used to accompany other dishes and include the mixed spices recipe you will need for many of the recipes.

- A wide range of these dishes contain pulses. Once you've cooked your pulses from scratch, you'll never go back to tins again; it takes time but no effort whatsoever. However, it's perfectly acceptable to use tinned pulses when you are pushed for time.

- Pulses such as beans and chickpeas have to be soaked overnight then boiled for roughly an hour. I tend to cook a whole batch, drain and freeze in individual portions, as all pulses freeze well. Lentils are an exception – you don't have to soak them, they take an hour or less to cook and unlike other pulses you can use the stock.
  Note: It's important to remember, never to add salt to pulses until they are well cooked.

- It's always best to soak rice for an hour before cooking.

- Quite a lot of the recipes include aubergines; when you buy them make sure they are firm and shiny.

- Tomatoes always taste better when kept out of the fridge at room temperature.

- Don't worry if you have leftovers; keep them in the fridge and the flavours will only improve.

ENJOY!

Dates grown on the coast

Introduction

Where my love of cooking began

When I was a young child growing up in Beirut, I used to watch my mother cooking with fascination, but she would not allow me to help because the kitchen was always so busy. Not only did she cook for our family, there were also regular visits from relatives who came to visit from our mountain village. Our house in the city was always open and welcoming to any visitors.

My mother, always a mountain woman even though she had moved to the city, remained a firm believer in cooking traditional, authentic food. She was a great cook and very resourceful with what she had learned, or sometimes with whatever was available in the house. She was not particularly adventurous and stuck to authentic and classic Lebanese recipes – and made them brilliantly.

As a child, I loved my trips with her to the food market in central Beirut, where she hunted for bargains and haggled for the best price. Mum would suddenly let go of my hand while she dived into heaps of vegetables to dig out the best from the bottom of the pile. When she visited England, she still tried to haggle – and sometimes succeeded!

The sudden death of my father, whom I worshipped, when I was fourteen meant that Mum was busier than ever and I was finally allowed in the kitchen to help. She trusted me to prepare a meal for the rest of the family. The more I cooked, the more I loved it. My mother never followed a recipe or ever read a recipe book: it was all built on remembering the flavours in the dishes.

Early life

I was born in the Chouf Mountains, a beautiful area, in a village called Gharifeh, south-east of Beirut, and grew up in a happy, loving home. Gharifeh, where the majority of the olive trees are pre-Roman, is known for its especially delicious olive oil. Most families there own land, where these ancient trees grow and from which people produce their own oil. Many still believe in growing their own vegetables too, making bread, tomato purée and *burghul* (bulgur or cracked wheat). It's a way of life that still continues, as it has for centuries, and for some people it's the only way to live a healthy life.

The population of our village is about 8,000 and it's just like one big extended family, as is the case in all rural towns in Lebanon. Hospitality and generosity are exceptional. My favourite aroma was, and still is, the late-summer quince and figs being made into thick jams full of chunky pieces that are served after a meal instead of a dessert. Walking around the village, I would also catch the aroma of tomatoes being cooked outdoors in the courtyards over wood fires for making tomato purée or the occasional scent of the soap that many people make from their own pure olive oil.

Cooking in the UK

I always loved cooking from a very young age, when, as I said, I observed my mother, who was a great cook with a very special touch. I also learnt a great deal from my grandmother, who lived with us until she died; she loved cooking and believed eating good food to be a pleasure.

When I came to England as a student, it was my first trip outside the Middle East. I had a real struggle with the food, until I discovered brown sauce: I splashed it on everything I ate! I started to cook Lebanese food, with whatever ingredients I could find, as at that time they were hard to source. Often I would invite friends round to share a tasty Lebanese meal and everyone enjoyed the food. Even on a restrictive student budget, I managed to produce tasty feasts at low cost, because so many Lebanese dishes are economical to make.

After getting married and running my own home, I never tired of cooking for my large family and frequently entertained friends over a Lebanese feast. As my five children were growing up, I ran Lebanese cooking classes in several adult education centres. The classes were very successful; the demand for places was high, and most of all they were lots of fun. While running them, I was often asked to write a cookery book, but it was something I never took seriously. After all, I am not a chef, nor have I ever worked in a restaurant. I only ever cooked in my own kitchen.

However, with my passion and love for Lebanese food, I had always wanted to share my recipes with as many people as possible. When my children had grown up and moved into their own homes, I set up a second home in Lebanon, so now divide my time between Lebanon and the UK. This made it possible for me to finally fulfil my ambition of writing my first book, *Everyday Lebanese Cooking*, and I was very happy with the result.

My first book included meat, poultry and fish recipes. When I was planning this book, I wondered how on earth I would find such a long list of vegetarian recipes. Some I rediscovered from my childhood; I also began to cook the forgotten dishes that are rarely cooked today, especially peasant food. Writing this book has been great fun, exploring beyond the usual everyday dishes. I have also enjoyed working hard to improve my photography. Every picture of a finished dish I simply photographed en route from the kitchen to the dinner table.

Basically, the majority of my recipes were learnt from my mother, grandmother and my aunts, who were all excellent cooks. Cooking Lebanese food is my passion and I hope you enjoy making and eating these wonderful dishes as much as I do.

Fresh almonds

CHAPTER 1

Lebanon and Its Food

Lebanese hospitality

In spite of the political instability, Lebanon is a fun-loving nation and its people continue to enjoy what the country has to offer: the beauty of nature, a great climate and, most importantly, good food. Throughout the Middle East, the Lebanese have the reputation of enjoying life to the full and taking every opportunity to do so. Eating plays a big part in that enjoyment. Food is the main focus of every occasion and it's socially important to gather round the table to share and enjoy it. We are always talking about food or eating food – often both.

The Lebanese are an extremely hospitable and loving people, and this is easily demonstrated by their approach to food. When a guest comes to the house, even if they are unexpected, they must be offered something to eat. If the guest refuses, they will be offered food again at regular intervals throughout the visit. The most useful thing you can learn is not to visit a Lebanese home with a full stomach because you will offend your host by refusing to eat or drink. Also, a Lebanese hostess will believe she has not provided enough food if everything is eaten, so they always prepare a larger quantity than is needed. After living in the UK for many years, I still feel uncomfortable if all the food is eaten.

Whenever I have friends from the UK and other countries visiting me in Lebanon, all my friends and family invite my guests into their homes for a feast of Lebanese dishes. They really do me proud with their exceptional hospitality and generosity. They would simply say they were 'sharing bread and salt'.

Maza is the main ritual of sharing a large number of dishes, especially when meeting with friends in restaurants. Everyone enjoys sharing small quantities of lots of different and interesting dishes. It usually starts with a cold *maza* followed by hot dishes. This is then followed by a substantial main course, with side dishes, all arranged in the centre of the table for people to help themselves. The Lebanese usually finish the meal with fresh fruit and coffee. Sweet dishes are very popular but eaten at different times rather than as part of the meal. It is normal to spend up to five hours in a restaurant!

Lebanese food and drink

The country's cuisine has evolved over the centuries, influenced by the climate, the agriculture, and by a number of invasions and outside influences. One of the biggest of those was the Ottoman Empire, which is why Lebanese food is so close to Turkish cuisine. Later, the Lebanese way of cooking was significantly refined by the occupation of the French.

A Druze lady selling home produce in the Chouf Mountains

For centuries, the people of the Middle East ate mostly vegetarian food. But the Lebanese continued to develop and refine the flavours and this has had a great influence on other cuisines in the Middle East. With its focus on herbs and spices, fresh fruit, vegetables, pulses and nuts, Lebanese cuisine is known as being the healthiest in the world. Natural flavours and freshness are the main attraction of the country's authentic vegetable dishes. These are enjoyed by all Lebanese, who are mostly non-vegetarian but enjoy many meat-free days.

The Lebanese eat a huge amount of vegetables and pulses, especially in the mountains where meat is not always available. You are usually judged for your Lebanese cooking skills by the standard of the traditional, authentic vegetable and pulse dishes you produce. Pulses are enjoyed as main dishes, dips and soup. Raw vegetables – such as lettuce, whole small cucumbers, cabbage, tomatoes, spring onions, carrots, green chillies and most of all fresh mint – are often presented on the table to be eaten on the side as condiments with whatever you are serving. Pickled vegetables are also very popular, particularly turnips, aubergines, cucumbers and chillies.

Nobody goes walking without a bag for foraging, as there is always something edible to be found. In winter and spring, country people often go off the beaten track to pick natural wild vegetables and herbs – such as mint and thyme (za'atar), leeks and asparagus. A variety of greens that are used in salads or as pastry fillings will also be collected. Wild fennel is also picked and used in making omelettes.

Olives are harvested in Lebanon between October and December. Every village has its own olive press and people take great pride in their olive oil. People pick their own olives then take the crop to the press, sitting and waiting for their turn until the oil is ready to take home. It's a seasonal ritual and a very sociable time of the year. I always used to laugh at my mother, as when eating out in restaurants, she would carry a small bottle of her own olive oil in her handbag. I now find myself following her tradition; it's true that every girl turns into her mother! The Lebanese eat a huge amount of olives. We enjoy them as snacks with bread as well as finishing the meal with a little bread and a few olives. When you switch to olives after a meal, it indicates that you have finished eating. I sometimes forget to put a bowl of olives on the table but people will always ask for it.

Olive oil, tomatoes and garlic are the main ingredients for cooking sauces, and used frequently. Many dishes are cooked in rich tomato sauce and mainly served with rice. Lebanese food is easy to prepare, extremely tasty, healthy and economical. You will find you can effortlessly turn a few ingredients into a very tasty meal.

Drinks

Arak is the Lebanese national drink, made from grapes and aniseed. It goes really well with Lebanese food and especially complements the lemony dishes. Commercial arak is 40 per cent alcohol and is usually diluted with two-thirds water or half arak to half water. It is always served with ice in a small glass.

Garlic sold on the roadside

Most country people grow vines and have a huge amount of grapes later in the summer. Many distil their own *arak* or use a local distiller, who will distil the *arak* three times for the best results. People take real pride in their *arak*, which is much stronger than the commercial equivalent and usually has more flavour. I am a big fan of home-distilled *arak* and I always choose to drink it with Lebanese food.

Lebanon claims to be the oldest site in the world for producing wine. Wine production in Lebanon was started 5,000 years ago when the Phoenicians, who were known for having the knowledge to produce the best wine, settled in Lebanon; the tradition was continued by the Romans. Just about all the major winemaking grapes are grown in the Bekaa Valley, which has 300 days a year of bright sunshine. Most of the wine produced in Lebanon is exported round the world, mainly where the Lebanese have settled.

The recipes

In this book, you will find a complete collection of Lebanese vegetarian dishes made with ingredients that are readily available in Western stores. Many recipes are so simple that you might think, 'I could do this without a book', but it's all about the right combination of flavours and ingredients. The majority of the recipes are the classic everyday dishes cooked in every Lebanese home; they are simple to make with the exception of a few that take longer to prepare but which are not difficult. You will also find authentic dishes that are no longer in common use. I have researched recipes from different parts of the country that were given to me by local people, and included those I thought delicious.

Most dishes are also suitable for vegans as it's not the norm to use dairy or eggs and only a few of my recipes include them. Christians in Lebanon take Lent weeks very seriously. The majority go completely vegan for the whole of the six weeks of Lent and therefore have an even wider repertoire of vegetarian dishes. My friend Colette manages to produce a different meal for her family without any repetition during this time and I am happy to be sharing some of her wonderful recipes in this book.

I have selected all the well-known traditional Lebanese dishes, from the rural mountains, to cities along the Mediterranean coast that stretches from the North to the South of the country. Also included are the most popular savoury and sweet street foods, including the familiar falafel wraps. In this book, you will find only authentic recipes that I was brought up on in Lebanon and which I made under the influence of my mother. I carried on the tradition, bringing up my own family on this healthy cuisine, a tradition they are now continuing with their own families.

Ingredients

Here is a guide to the most commonly used ingredients in Lebanese cuisine. Most ingredients are always available in UK shops and supermarkets. However, there are four to five ingredients that you may or may not find in a supermarket. These can be bought in Middle Eastern stores or online. Note that these are not commonly used ingredients and mostly used for sweets and desserts. Once you have them, they will keep for a long time.

AUBERGINES are the most versatile vegetable, and they are used in so many different dishes; they are popular, low-cost and keep well for several days. When there are aubergines in the house, you can always create a simple tasty meal, snack or dips.

BREAD. As well as being the main source of carbohydrate, most people in Lebanon have bread with whatever they are eating.

BURGHUL (bulgur or cracked wheat). This is the main ingredient in Lebanese national dishes such as *tabouleh* and *kebbeh*. *Burghul* is also used in other ways and sometimes as a substitute for rice. In the recipes here, I used wholewheat brown *burghul* but if it is not available use white *burghul*, which is often sold in Western supermarkets – *Burghul* is available either coarsely or finely ground; I specify which one to use.

CANDIED ORANGE PETALS. These are only used with some sweet recipes; they are extremely sweet but used for decorating and to add colour to a dish.

CINNAMON. This is the most frequently added spice in Lebanese cooking, but seeing it in some recipes can come as a shock to Westerners, who are less likely to use cinnamon in savoury dishes.

CORIANDER. This herb is used in many cooked dishes. Most people are familiar with the distinctive flavour of coriander.

CUMIN. We don't use many spices in Lebanese cooking but cumin is used in many dishes, either whole or ground. Also, it is believed to be healthy: in my hometown, cumin is frequently given to women for several weeks after giving birth.

GARLIC. This is added in large quantities. You may find it a little scary when you see just how much is used in some of the recipes, but you'll be surprised how well it integrates into the dish.

LEMONS. These are also used in large quantities. Many of the dishes are very lemony, but the quantity may be reduced to suit your taste.

MINT. It is often used, dried or fresh. Even when it's not included in a recipe, mint is frequently served as a condiment with many dishes.

MISKEH. Commonly used in Greek food, this is also known as mystic or mastic gum. *Miskeh* is a resin extracted from tree bark that is usually sold in the form of small, hard crystals. In Lebanon it is only used in some milky desserts, although it is optional. Apart from having a fabulous flavour, *miskeh* is a cure for stomach pain as it kills bacteria. As with

Lemons

Sumac

mazaher, it can be bought in Middle Eastern shops or online. *Miskeh* is an expensive ingredient but you only need to use very little and it keeps indefinitely.

MOUNEH (preserves). Country people store preserves such as *burghul*, jams, olive oil, pickles, za'atar, sumac and all the pulses year round. Apart from choosing to have home-made *mouneh*, they enjoy the ritual of making it.

NUTS. A variety of nuts are used in both savoury and sweet dishes, mainly pine nuts, almonds, walnuts and pistachios.

12

*Orange blossom water (*mazaher*)*

OLIVE OIL. The most used oil in Lebanese cuisine. As well as for cooking, it is often drizzled on food. All oil in Lebanon is extra virgin olive oil. It is important to use good-quality oil for both cooking and dressing.

ONIONS. Used very frequently, sometimes in large quantities.

ORANGE BLOSSOM WATER (*mazaher*). I always believed this was made from any citrus fruit blossoms until recently when I learnt that only Seville orange blossoms are used in the distillation of *mazaher*. When I went to Saida (Sidon), the capital city of the South, which is known as the citrus fruit county, I bought a few kilos of blossoms to take back to a friend's distillery in my village, who offered to make it for me. It is a novelty, of course, to have it homemade, but I am usually happy to buy it ready-made. *Mazaher* is only used in sweet dishes and is extremely strong in flavour, but it is a very important ingredient. It is essential to buy the real *mazaher* and not the essence or concentrate in a little bottle. This can be bought in Middle Eastern shops, some supermarkets or online.

Note: It is very important to use only the amount suggested in the recipes, as adding too much will ruin your dessert. Make sure you only use orange blossom water.

PARSLEY. This is frequently added to savoury dishes. Whenever I went to a particular greengrocer in the UK to buy a large quantity of parsley, mainly for *tabouleh*, I would notice the curious look on his face, as if to say, 'How could anyone use so much parsley?'

POMEGRANATE MOLASSES. Made from the concentrated juice of pomegranates, this thick, dark syrup is added to some sauces or dressings. Many people use it as frequently as others would tomato ketchup.

PULSES. All the different kinds of beans, lentils and especially chickpeas are used at least twice a week in one way or another – in dips, as hummus, cooked with other ingredients, in soups and served hot with lemon dressing. Chickpeas are also popular when fresh; the chickpea is picked out of the pod and eaten like a nut.

RICE. Served with all sorts of stews and other rice dishes. When my children were growing up, they suffered withdrawal symptoms if I didn't cook rice for two or three days.

ROSE WATER (*maward*). As with *mazaher*, this is only used in sweet dishes and sometimes to make a syrupy drink. You can even buy rose-water sorbet.

SUMAC. In recent years, sumac has become known in the West and can be bought in some supermarkets. It is the fruit of the Mediterranean sumac tree. Dark

Miskeh (mystic)

Fresh chickpeas

14

maroon in colour, it tastes lemony and is therefore usually used instead of, or along with, lemon for its distinctive flavour. Some prefer to sprinkle sumac on salads, fried eggs, or sometimes to serve it with olive oil on sliced tomatoes.

TAHINI (sesame cream). The popularity of hummus, a rich dish made mostly with chickpeas and tahini, has introduced many people to the flavour. Tahini is a common ingredient in our cuisine, used as a sauce in many dishes, and I really hope you will enjoy the experience of using it. Always use light tahini rather than the whole dark tahini.

TOMATOES. Apart from being added to many salads and served as a condiment with many dishes, sauces used in cooking are often made from tomatoes.

ZA'ATAR. Sometimes called wild thyme in the West, if you can get it from Middle Eastern shops or online, using *za'atar* is better than substituting thyme. You can buy it either plain or mixed with sumac and roasted sesame seeds. If you have both *za'atar* and sumac in your cupboard, they will keep for over a year.

Za'atar

Opposite: pomegranates

CHAPTER 2

Dips and Starters

Maza

Often translated as 'starters', *maza,* the tradition of sharing a large number of dishes with friends and family, is the best part of a Lebanese meal. The food is scooped up with a piece of bread, so it is always essential to have plenty on the table. Often the person sitting next to you will tear off a piece of your bread for dipping, if it happens to be close by. Don't be offended; in Lebanon it is normal to share food.

With the broad selection of dishes served, a *maza* is always enjoyable. In restaurants, mains are never ordered until everyone has finished with the *maza,* as it's often more than enough. The meal normally starts with *tabouleh* or *fattoush* and then cold dishes followed by hot ones. You are never rushed as long as there is still food on the table.

Sometimes at home we serve a main dish or two at the same time as the *maza* before the guests are too full. Hours pass by while eating, chatting, drinking and exchanging stories. Eating in Lebanon is very much a prolonged social event.

Herb and Bulgur Wheat Salad
Tabouleh

Tabouleh is the most popular traditional dish in Lebanon. Apart from being one of the healthiest foods, you will never tire of eating it. It's served as a starter, for snacks, and for afternoon tea followed by other sweet cakes and pastries. Basically, *tabouleh* is served on every occasion where food is required.

SERVES 4

200g finely chopped parsley, with end stalks removed

30g finely chopped fresh mint

$\frac{1}{4}$ tsp ground black pepper (optional)

70g (1 small) onion, chopped

500g tomatoes, finely diced, 1 tbsp reserved

50ml lemon juice

100ml olive oil

1 level tsp salt

25g fine *burghul* (bulgur wheat)

Preparation time: 30 minutes

- Rinse the parsley and mint and allow to drain in a colander.

- Meanwhile, rub the ground pepper, if using, with the onions, using your fingers (doing this stops the onion from smelling stronger after chopping).

- Combine the onions with the tomatoes in a bowl.

- Add the lemon juice, oil, salt, parsley and mint.

- Add the *burghul* and mix all the ingredients well.

- Garnish with the reserved tomato and serve with lettuce or tender cabbage leaves on the side.

Cook's tip
- You can do all the chopping in advance. Add the dressing and the *burghul* just before serving.

Pitta Crouton Salad

Fattoush

There are no restrictions in the use of ingredients when making *fattoush*. You can use whatever you have in the fridge or leave out what doesn't suit your palate, as long as it isn't the bread and mint. During the month of Ramadan, *fattoush* is always served at the beginning of the meal.

SERVES 4

25g chopped mint leaves
400g tomatoes, chopped
200g cucumber, diced
80g spring onions, trimmed
  and chopped
6 sliced radishes
1 medium green or red
  pepper, deseeded and
  chopped
140g lettuce leaves (cos or
  iceberg), thinly sliced
150g toasted pitta bread
2 heaped tsp sumac
2 cloves garlic, crushed
50ml lemon juice or wine
  vinegar
50ml olive oil
1 tsp salt
50–70g pomegranate seeds
  (optional)

Preparation time: 30 minutes

• Place all the prepared ingredients in a large bowl and mix together.

• Taste for salt and lemon, adding more if needed, as some people prefer it sharp and lemony.

• Serve as a starter.

Cook's tip
• It is always easier to prepare *fattoush* in advance and add the toasted bread and dressing just before serving. Sometimes we substitute lemon juice with wine vinegar.

Roasted Aubergine Dip

Baba Ghanouj

This is one of the most popular dips and always enjoyed by everyone. The smoky taste of the aubergines combined with the lemon and tahini is just magical.

SERVES 4–6

2 large aubergines
50ml tahini
2 cloves garlic, crushed
1 tsp salt
Juice of 1 lemon
20ml cold water

To garnish
Pomegranate seeds or
  chopped mint leaves
A sprinkle of chilli powder or
  paprika (optional)
A little olive oil, to drizzle
  (optional)

Preparation time: 15 minutes
Cooking time: 20 minutes

- Place the aubergines on the flame of the gas burner on the hob, turning them occasionally and making sure top and bottom ends are soft and well cooked. If you prefer not to have the smoky taste that you get from cooking over a flame, or have an electric hob, prick the aubergines and roast in a preheated oven at 220°C/425°F/gas mark 7 for about 20 minutes.

- Peel the aubergines and rinse off any remaining skin, then mash by hand (avoid using a food processor).

- Add the remaining ingredients and combine well.

- Turn onto a serving dish and garnish with pomegranate seeds, if available, or a few chopped mint leaves, and sprinkle with chilli or paprika for colour. Drizzle with a little olive oil.

- Serve with pitta bread.

Cook's tip
- Aubergines discolour quickly. If you are not using them soon after cooking, and are planning to prepare the dish later, add the lemon juice to the peeled aubergines to prevent this from happening.

Chilli Mixed Peppers

Harrah

This is a great dish to serve as a starter or dip. It's really tasty and although not commonly made at home by the Lebanese, it is often served in restaurants. Whenever I serve it, I get lots of compliments.

SERVES 4–6

100ml olive oil
230g (1 large) onion, finely
  chopped
4 cloves garlic, chopped
2 red and green chillis,
  deseeded and finely
  chopped
550g mixed peppers,
  deseeded and diced
20g chopped fresh coriander
1 tsp salt

Preparation time: 15 minutes
Cooking time: 35 minutes

• Heat the oil and fry the onion until it turns golden to light brown.

• Add the garlic and chilli and continue to cook, stirring, for a couple of minutes.

• Add the peppers and mix well. Cook on low heat for about 20 minutes, turning occasionally, until the peppers look well sautéed and there is no liquid in the pan.

• Finally, add the coriander and salt and cook for another two minutes.

• Serve cold with bread and lemon wedges.

Avocado and Bulgur Wheat Dip

Kebbeh Avocado

Kebbeh is a Lebanese national dish. It is prepared in so many different ways, with pumpkin, fish and mostly meat, but this is another vegetarian version. *Kebbeh* balls are often served with *maza* (starters). I just couldn't imagine what it would taste like as although I'd heard of it, I'd never tried it until .I began writing this book. To my surprise I loved it and now always serve it as one of my main starters with *maza*.

SERVES 4

50g *burghul* (bulgur wheat)
50g spring onions, trimmed
  and finely chopped
3 medium-sized ripe
  avocados, mashed
1¹/₂ tsp marjoram
¹/₂ tsp salt
¹/₂ tsp ground black pepper
1 tsp dried mint
1 tsp ground cumin
50g chopped walnuts, for
  topping

Preparation time: 10–15
  minutes

• Rinse the *burghul*, drain all the water and set aside while you prepare the rest of the ingredients.

• Add the spring onions to the mashed avocados in a large bowl, along with the herbs and spices.

• Now add the soaked *burghul* to the mixture and mix well.

• Scoop out onto a serving dish and scatter the walnuts over the top.

• Garnish with fresh mint, if available. Serve with toasted strips of pitta bread within two hours, as the avocados may begin to discolour.

Cook's tip
• Always rinse, drain well and leave the *burghul* to soak. Never leave it in water, otherwise it will become soggy and mushy.

Chickpeas with Tahini Dip

Hummus

Hummus has become so international that you can now find it in almost every shop or supermarket. It's so easy to make and you'll never buy it ready-made again once you've tasted this homemade version.

SERVES 4–6

250g cooked (125g dried)
  chickpeas (page xi)
100g tahini
2 cloves garlic, crushed
Juice of 1$\frac{1}{2}$ lemons
1 tsp salt
Chopped parsley, to garnish

Preparation time: 15
  minutes, plus soaking
  overnight
Cooking time: 1 hour, to
  cook chickpeas

• After making sure the chickpeas are well cooked and feel a bit mushy, place in a food processor or blender and process until they form a smooth paste.

• Turn into a bowl. Add the tahini, garlic, lemon juice and salt and mix well. Add a little water as you stir, as it will look very thick and dry in texture. Mix until you have a creamy consistency.

• Spread the hummus onto a serving plate and garnish with chopped parsley and whatever else you prefer (see tip below).

• Serve with pitta bread.

Cook's tip
• You may also garnish this dish with chopped tomatoes, sliced radishes, spring onions, olives or a few chickpeas. A sprinkle of ground chilli adds flavour and colour.

Smoky Aubergines with Lemon and Garlic Dressing

Salata Raheb

Although this dish is referred to as salad, it is always served as a starter or part of a *maza*. The dominant smoky aubergine taste is delicious. Whenever I want to have a light-eating day, I go for this flavoursome salad with a little bread, as although light, it satisfies my hunger.

SERVES 4

2 large aubergines
1 small to medium onion, chopped
Juice of 1 lemon
200g (2 small) tomatoes, chopped
1–2 cloves garlic, crushed
1 level tsp salt
A little chopped parsley, to garnish
A little olive oil, to drizzle
Lemon wedges, to serve

Preparation time: 10 minutes
Cooking time: 20 minutes

- For a smoky taste, roast the whole aubergines on the flame of a gas hob for about 20 minutes, turning occasionally, until they are soft.

- When they are cool enough to handle, peel off the skin then rinse under a cold tap to remove any remaining skin.

- Chop the aubergine and place in a bowl. Add the onion, lemon juice, tomatoes, garlic and salt.

- Turn out onto a serving dish, sprinkle parsley over the top and drizzle with olive oil.

- Serve with pitta bread and lemon wedges.

Cook's tip
- This dish is supposed to have the lovely smoky flavour that cooking over a flame gives, but if you only have an electric hob, you can cook the aubergines in an oven preheated to 220°C/425°F/gas mark 7 for about 20 minutes. Prick the aubergines with a fork before roasting.

Yogurt Cream Cheese with Vegetables
Labneh Ma Khoodra

Once you've made *labneh* (page 262) and seen how easy it is to make, you'll never be without it in your fridge. It's also incredibly versatile. Here, a few tasty ingredients have been added to make it into an especially tasty dip.

SERVES 4

80g black olives, preferably pitted
½ red pepper, deseeded and diced
½ green pepper, deseeded and diced
50–60g (1 small) onion, chopped
15g chopped fresh mint
1 clove garlic, crushed
½ tsp salt
400g *labneh* (page 262)
Olive oil, for drizzling

Preparation time: 10 minutes

- Remove the stones from the olives and cut them into quarters. (You'll get much more flavour this way than buying pitted olives.)

- Combine with the peppers, onion and mint.

- In a separate bowl, mix the garlic and salt with the *labneh*.

- Add the vegetables to the *labneh* and mix well.

- Transfer to a serving dish and drizzle with olive oil.

- Serve with strips of toasted pitta bread.

Cook's tip
- This dish looks lovely garnished with a few whole black olives and some chopped fresh mint. It makes a perfect snack spread inside pitta bread or a baguette and then lightly toasted.

Chilli and Nut Mix

Mhammara

The Lebanese are not a nation of hot chilli lovers, although there is some fairly hot food around, thanks to the historic presence of Armenians in Lebanon, who introduced us to hot food. I always enjoyed this dish, which is normally served only in restaurants, but didn't find many versions that suited my taste. I was very grateful, therefore, to get this recipe from a kind chef who in my opinion made the best *mhammara*.

SERVES 6

40g almonds
70g cashews
30g walnuts
30 hazelnuts
6 water biscuits
1 red pepper, deseeded
1 whole red chilli, deseeded
1 tsp paprika
1 tsp ground chilli
$\frac{1}{2}$ tsp salt
$\frac{1}{2}$ tsp ground cumin
60ml olive oil
A few halved walnuts, to
  garnish

Preparation time: 15 minutes

• Put all the nuts and biscuits in a food processor and chop until the texture resembles breadcrumbs but remains coarse. Transfer to a mixing bowl.

• Also in the food processor, blend the pepper and whole chilli together with the paprika, ground chilli, salt, cumin and oil, then sprinkle over the nuts.

• Mix all the ingredients together with a spoon, transfer to a serving plate and garnish with walnuts.

• Serve with bread.

Cook's tip
• Sometimes this dish is made mild with less chilli, if preferred, and it still tastes just as good. You can use a few slices of deseeded mild chilli to garnish if you wish.

Tahini and Onion Dip

Tagen

This easy-to-make tahini dip is often served as part of a *maza* (starters) spread. It's served cold and can therefore be prepared in advance.

SERVES 4–6

100ml corn or sunflower oil
400g onions, halved then
 sliced (2 large)
150g tahini
50ml fresh lemon juice (1
 medium juicy lemon)
700ml cold water
1 tsp salt

To garnish
A little chopped parsley
A little chilli powder

Preparation time: 10 minutes
Cooking time: 30–40
 minutes

• Heat the oil and sauté the onions until they soften and are slightly browned. Leave in the pan.

• Mix the tahini and lemon juice together in a bowl until thick and fluffy.

• Gradually add the water to the mixture, and keep stirring, until it is the consistency of thin cream without lumps.

• Add the tahini sauce and salt to the onions in the pan.

• Heat, while stirring, until the mix starts to bubble, then reduce the heat to low, stirring occasionally, until the tahini starts to separate. Leave to cool.

• Transfer to a serving dish and garnish with chopped parsley and a sprinkle of chilli powder.

• This dish is delicious served with pitta bread and plenty of lemon wedges on the side.

Broad Bean Dip with Goat Cheese
Mtabal Foul

This is not a very common dish and therefore everyone prepares it in a different way. I have tried different variations but this is my favourite. This recipe is simple and flavoursome, made in 15 minutes from start to finish.

SERVES 4

500g frozen broad beans, or
   fresh, podded, if available
2–3 cloves garlic, crushed
Juice of 1 juicy lemon
10g chopped mint leaves
1 tsp salt
125g soft goat's cheese,
   without rind
Olive oil, for drizzling

Preparation time: 10 minutes
Cooking time: 5 minutes

• Bring a pan of water to the boil and cook the beans for 5 minutes, then drain and allow to cool.

• Place the beans in a food processor or blender and process to a rough purée.

• Tip the purée into a large bowl and mix in the crushed garlic, lemon juice, chopped mint and salt.

• Scoop onto a serving dish, crumble the cheese with the tips of your fingers over the top of the broad beans. Drizzle with a little olive oil.

• Serve with toasted pitta bread and fresh mint leaves as a condiment.

Cook's tip
• With the huge variety of dips and starters in Lebanon, this dish doesn't tend to get served very often, but it is equally as good as the others. You can sprinkle it with a little paprika just before serving to give it more colour.

Cheese Rolls
Rakakat Jibneh

Cheese rolls are often served together with other pastries and small *kebbeh* balls, either with starters or at buffets. Normally they are deep-fried but I prefer to bake them. They are ideal for freezing and cook better straight from the freezer.

MAKES 15

1 packet frozen filo pastry
200g feta cheese
10g chopped parsley
70g butter, melted

Preparation time: 30 minutes
Cooking time: 25 minutes

• Preheat the oven to 180°C/350°F/gas mark 4.

• Mix together the feta cheese and parsley in a bowl.

• Cut the filo sheets into halves and brush each sheet with melted butter.

• Place 2 teaspoons of the cheese mix onto each filo half and spread over the middle part of the diagonal; fold the top end over the cheese, then the sides and continue to roll to the end (see photos).

• Place the rolls on a greased baking tray, leaving a space between each one.

• Brush with butter and bake in the preheated oven for 25 minutes.

• Serve warm.

Wild Thyme or Sumac Bread

Khibez Bzaatar/Summac

To be honest, I've only ever had this in a restaurant when they put a pile of the crispy bread on the table to nibble at while I decided what to order. It was so delicious on its own or to use for dipping that since then I've made it at home many times and everyone loves it. Good quality *za'atar* and sumac can be bought in supermarkets, specialist shops or online. Lebanese bread is similar to the pitta bread you can buy from Middle Eastern stores and supermarkets. Pitta bread is a good substitute for all dishes where Lebanese bread is called for.

SERVES 4–6

6 loaves Lebanese bread
100ml olive oil
15g sumac
30g *za'atar* (or thyme)

Preparation time: 10 minutes
Cooking time: 15–20
  minutes

• As you will see from the photo, this bread splits into two pieces. After splitting each loaf, brush the inside of each half with olive oil.

• Sprinkle each half with either sumac or *za'atar*.

• Toast all the bread pieces on the cut sides only, either in the oven at 220°C/425°F/gas mark 7, or under the grill, until brown and crispy.

• Serve the stack with dips or just for nibbling before serving a main meal.

Cook's tip
• If toasting this bread under a grill, keep close eye on it as it only takes a short time to toast and can therefore burn very quickly.

Aubergine Pizza

Pizza Batingane Meshwi

This recipe requires very little effort and usually goes down really well with guests while you're busy putting the final touches to your main meal before serving.

SERVES 4

1 large aubergine
1 tbsp olive oil
2 cloves garlic, chopped
400g tomatoes, diced
1 tsp dried basil
Salt, to taste
100g feta cheese, crumbled
Few basil leaves, to garnish

Preparation time: 10 minutes
Cooking time: 30 minutes

• Slice the aubergine into 1cm thick slices and roast in an oven preheated to 220°C/425°F/gas mark 7 or on a griddle to brown and become a little crispy.

• Heat the oil and fry the garlic for few seconds then add the tomatoes, basil and salt. Simmer until the sauce becomes thick.

• Place the aubergine slices on a baking tray, spread tomato sauce over each one and top with feta cheese.

• Place under a preheated grill until the cheese is slightly browned.

• Transfer to a serving plate and garnish with basil leaves.

• Serve warm.

CHAPTER 3

Soups and Salads

Shawraba Wa Salatat

There are already so many books filled with delicious soup recipes, so I decided to include just a few key Lebanese recipes, which are very tasty, filling and nutritious.

Soup is rarely served as a starter in Lebanon and more often as a meal. When you try these hearty traditional soups you'll see why.

Here you'll also find a huge variety of salads, either to serve as side dishes, to include as part of a *maza* or to serve at the beginning of a meal. Some are vegetable salads and others are made with pulses. In one form or another, in Lebanon at least one kind of salad is always served with every meal. Dry dishes in particular, which don't include a sauce, are always accompanied by salad, a yogurt dressing or both.

Mixed Pulses Thick Soup

Makhlouta

This mountain peasant soup is one of the very traditional recipes. It is never served as a starter, as with a satisfying combination of pulses it is extremely filling. *Makhlouta* is a very wintery dish; on cold days, people huddle round the fire, which is also used as a stove, and get the *makhlouta* going.

SERVES 6

100g dried kidney beans
100g dried flageolet beans
100g dried haricot beans
100g dried chickpeas
100g dried green lentils
500g (3 medium) onions,
　coarsely chopped
100ml olive oil
2^1/$_2$ tsp ground cumin
2 tsp ground cinnamon
^{1}/$_2$ tsp ground black pepper
1^1/$_2$ tsp salt
80g coarse *burghul* (bulgur
　wheat)

Preparation time: 10
　minutes, plus soaking
　overnight
Cooking time: 1^1/$_2$ hours

- Combine all the beans and chickpeas (but not the lentils) in a large pan and leave to soak overnight in plenty of water, unless using tinned pulses.

- Drain the soaking water, replace with fresh and bring to a boil; turn down the heat and cook the combination for about an hour. Drain well.

- Meanwhile, cook the lentils separately in 1 litre of water, then add with their stock to the pulses.

- While all the pulses are cooking, fry the onions in the olive oil to brown slightly. Add the spices and salt and stir for 1 minute.

- Add the onions together with the *burghul* to the pulses and allow to cook for another 15–20 minutes.

- Serve with bread if required.

Cook's tip
- For this dish, there are no restrictions on how many kinds of beans you use. It tastes even better if cooked a few hours before serving, when all the beans and pulses will absorb the flavours.

Lemony Lentil with Chard or Spinach Soup

Adas Bhamoud

With just a few ingredients, this soup is always a favourite in Lebanon and whoever tasted it at my house in England added it to their repertoire. As young children, my mother often made this soup because we loved it so much that we ate it as our main meal.

SERVES 4

250g green or brown lentils,
　　plus 1.5ltr water
400g (2 large) onions
100ml olive oil
500g chard leaves and stalks
　　(or spinach if not
　　available), chopped
Juice of 2 juicy lemons
1–2 tsp salt

Preparation time: 15 minutes
Cooking time: 1 hour

- Place the lentils in the water and bring to the boil, then turn down the heat and simmer for 40 minutes.

- While the lentils are cooking, chop the onions and fry in 50ml of the olive oil to brown and add to lentils.

- Add the chopped chard leaves and stalks or spinach to the lentils and cook for a further 15–20 minutes.

- Taste the lentils to make sure they are well cooked before adding the lemon juice and salt. Remove from the heat and add the remaining olive oil.

- Serve hot or just at room temperature.

Cook's tip
- If using chard, make sure you use the stalks as they add a lot to the flavour and texture.

Split Lentil Soup
Shawraba Adas

This soup is simple, full of flavour and economical. In the old days it was always served with school dinners because it is low cost and nutritious, but as kids we never tired of eating it – and indeed still regularly eat it.

SERVES 4

350g orange split lentils, plus
   1 ltr water
50ml olive oil
300g (2 medium) onions,
   chopped
1 tsp ground cumin
1/2 tsp cinnamon
Juice of 1 lemon (optional)
1 tsp salt

Preparation time: 5 minutes
Cooking time: 45 minutes

• Rinse the lentils and place in the water in a large pan (adding no salt at this stage).

• Bring to the boil, then turn the heat down to avoid boiling over and simmer for 20 minutes. The lentils should look quite mushy. Keep an eye on them and add more water when necessary.

• While the lentils are cooking, heat the oil and fry the onions until golden brown. Add the cumin and cinnamon and stir for 1 minute.

• Add the onion mixture to the lentils and cook for another 10 minutes.

• Finally, add the lemon juice and salt.

• Serve with bread.

Cook's tip
• You can vary this soup by adding chopped tomatoes, carrots or diced peppers. Sometimes I add roasted chopped peppers, which makes it very special.

Vegetable Soup

Showraba Khoudra

This is another filling soup that combines vegetables and protein. There are no rules on what vegetables you can use; whatever you choose, you will still get a good combination of flavours.

SERVES 4–6

200g split orange lentils
50ml olive oil
250g (1 very large) onion, chopped
1 tsp ground cinnamon
2 tsp ground cumin
350g white turnips, cut into small cubes (if in season)
300g carrots, diced
200g courgettes, cut into cubes
1 small red pepper, deseeded and chopped
1 small green pepper, deseeded and chopped
300g tomatoes, chopped
1–2 tsp salt
Juice of 1 lemon (optional)

Preparation time: 15 minutes
Cooking time: 45 minutes

- Rinse the lentils and cook in boiling water for about 20 minutes.

- Meanwhile, heat the oil and fry the onion to brown. Add the cinnamon and cumin and stir for 1 or 2 minutes then add the mixture to the lentils.

- Add all the other prepared vegetables, tomatoes, salt and lemon juice, if using, and cook for another 30 minutes until the soup is fairly thick.

- Serve with bread and lemon wedges. A little chilli sauce drizzled over each serving is also delicious.

Green Bean Salad

Salata Loubeyeh

The Lebanese love their salads. As I said earlier, there will always be some kind of salad present on the table. Apart from green salads, you will often be served pulses. This salad is frequently served as part of a dinner spread and it is sometimes eaten on its own with a piece of bread.

SERVES 4

700g green beans
100g (1 small) onion, chopped
30g chopped flat parsley
40ml olive oil
Juice of 1 lemon
2 cloves garlic, crushed
1 tsp salt

Preparation time: 10 minutes
Cooking time: 10 minutes

• Trim the beans, cut into small pieces and boil with a little salt for 10 minutes or less, depending on the variety.

• Drain the beans, rinse in cold water to prevent further cooking and allow to drain well.

• Add the onion and parsley to the beans and mix well.

• To make the dressing, blend together the olive oil, lemon juice, garlic and salt; add to the salad and stir through.

• This dish adds a lot to a salad selection, or it can be served with any of the rice dishes. It's also delicious eaten together with potato salad.

Cook's tip
• You can add cubes of boiled potato to the beans, which is a lovely combination.

Wild Rocket, Aubergine and Halloumi Salad

Salata Roca Whaloum

In this salad you get all sorts of strong flavours from all the ingredients. Easy to make, it can be served as a starter or as a snack or light lunch.

SERVES 4

200g (1 large) aubergine, cut into 1cm thick slices
150g cherry tomatoes, cut in half
100g wild rocket (*roca*)
100g halloumi cheese, thinly sliced
1 tbsp olive oil
2 tbsp balsamic vinegar

Preparation time: 5 minutes
Cooking time: 15 minutes

• Heat a griddle or a heavy-based frying pan and brown the aubergine on both sides.

• Mix the tomatoes and rocket in a serving dish, place the browned aubergine slices over the top and then the halloumi.

• Blend the oil with the vinegar. Pour over the top or serve as a dressing on the side, as some people prefer.

• Serve straight away with bread.

Cabbage Salad

Salata Malfoof

This simple cabbage salad is very special and it's also economical to make. However, you need a certain type of cabbage with a tender leaf. In Lebanon there's only one variety that is sweet and tender. Here, I would recommend Sweetheart or January King.

SERVES 4

450g tender white cabbage, cut into shreds
Juice of 1 lemon
50ml olive oil
1 or two cloves garlic, crushed
$^1/_2$ tsp salt

Preparation time: 10–15 minutes

• Wash the cabbage and allow to drain completely.

• Make a dressing by blending the lemon juice, olive oil, garlic and salt.

• Add the dressing to the shredded cabbage and mix well.

• Allow to stand for 5–10 minutes before serving.

• This popular salad goes with many dishes, especially *Mjadra* (page 204) and *Burghul Ma'A Banadoura* (page 90).

Green Beans and Butter Bean Salad
Salata Loubeyeh Ma Fasoulia

For presentation and flavour, this combination of two beans with a refreshing traditional Lebanese dressing topped with walnuts is unbeatable.

SERVES 4

200g green beans
50ml olive oil
Juice of 1 lemon
1 clove garlic, chopped
$^1/_2$ tsp salt
30g chopped walnuts
300g cooked (150g dried) butter beans

Preparation time: 10 minutes
Cooking time: 10 minutes for butter beans; see page xi if using dried butter beans

• Blanche the green beans for a few minutes depending on the variety you use and whether you prefer them well cooked or al dente. Allow to cool and then drain well.

• Make a dressing by mixing the oil, lemon juice, garlic and salt.

• Reserving a few walnuts, combine the remainder with the green beans and butter beans in a bowl, add the dressing and stir well.

• Sprinkle reserved walnuts over the top.

• Serve as part of a salad spread or buffet.

Cook's tip
• Walnuts are very important in this recipe as they complement the flavour of the beans.

Beetroot Salad with Yogurt and Tahini Sauce

Salata Shamandar

I've lived on Lebanese food all my life. With the huge variety of dishes in this cuisine I am constantly exploring and finding recipes I never even knew existed, such as this salad. Beetroots are often chopped and mixed in with other greens, but never in the way they are in this recipe.

SERVES 4

500g cooked beetroot
2 cloves garlic, crushed
$\frac{1}{2}$ tsp salt
100ml tahini
200ml natural yogurt, plus
  extra to thin
1 tsp dried mint, to garnish

Preparation time: 10 minutes
Cooking time: 30–40
  minutes, if using fresh
  beetroot

• Peel the beetroot if using fresh and cut into small cubes.

• Mix the garlic and salt with the tahini.

• Gradually add yogurt to the tahini mixture, blending to form quite a thick sauce. If it's too thick, add a little more yogurt.

• Add the sauce to the beetroot and turn to coat all the cubes.

• Transfer to a serving dish and sprinkle with dried mint.

• Serve as an additional salad or with omelettes.

Cook's tip
• Choose firm beetroot, then trim any leaves 2–3cm above the beet to minimise the dark juices bleeding. Wash gently. Place in a pan of warm water, bring to the boil and simmer for 20–30 minutes until tender. Leave to cool.

Quinoa and Herb Salad

Quinoa Tabouleh

When visiting a friend a couple of years ago, she served me this salad, which I thoroughly enjoyed. It was my first experience of eating quinoa and I've made it so many times since then.

SERVES 4

150g quinoa, plus 350ml
  water
50g chopped parsley
10g chopped mint
200g tomatoes, chopped
90g cucumber (optional),
  diced
50g spring onions, trimmed
  and chopped
Juice of 1 lemon
2 tbsp olive oil
½ tsp salt

Preparation time: 10–15
  minutes
Cooking time: 20 minutes

• Rinse and drain the quinoa and put it in a pan with the water. Bring to the boil, turn the heat down, cover and simmer until all the water has evaporated. Transfer to a large bowl and leave to cool.

• Wash and drain the parsley and mint.

• Combine all the ingredients with the quinoa and stir well.

• Serve as a starter or snack on its own.

Cook's tips
• Quinoa has only been introduced to the Lebanese in recent years, so this recipe is a modern one.

• You can prepare all the ingredients in advance, adding the lemon, oil and salt just before serving.

Lemony Potato Salad

Salata Batata

This isn't just another potato salad. The combination of lemon, garlic and mint gives it a deliciously fresh flavour.

SERVES 4–5

1kg potatoes, peeled and cut
  into large chunks
250g (1 large) red onion,
  finely diced
Juice of 1 large lemon
2 cloves garlic, crushed
1 tsp salt
50ml olive oil
25g chopped fresh mint

Preparation time: 15 minutes
Cooking time: 15 minutes

• Cook the potatoes in boiling water and salt for 15 minutes, making sure not to overcook them.

• Drain the potatoes and set aside to cool while preparing the dressing.

• In a large bowl combine the onion, lemon juice, garlic, salt, olive oil and mint.

• Cut the cooked potatoes into small cubes, add to the dressing and mix to coat.

• Serve as part of a salad buffet or with either of the egg omelettes in Chapter 4.

Cook's tip
• Sometimes chopped parsley is used instead of the chopped mint. It's a matter of preference.

Tahini Salad

Salata Tarator

This is made with the basic tahini sauce but you can turn it into a special sauce or salad (see Cook's Tip). Tahini is something that's always served in one form or another.

SERVES 4

100ml light tahini
Juice of 1 lemon
I clove garlic, crushed
$^1/_2$ tsp salt
120ml cold water
400g tomatoes, chopped
50g chopped flat parsley

Preparation time: 15 minutes

- Follow the tahini sauce (*tarator*) instructions (page 266) using the quantities listed here.

- Add the tomatoes and parsley and mix together.

- Serve with Cumin Rice (page 269) or roasted vegetables.

Cook's tip
- Sometimes I like to add a little chilli powder to this recipe. And literally eat it on its own scooped with a piece of bread.

Minty Yogurt and Cucumber Salad

Laban Be Kheyar

Yogurt is often used as a dressing in one way or another. Always have a bowl of yogurt on the table as a side dish. Many people are familiar with this salad and sometimes it is also served as a dip.

SERVES 4

1 clove garlic, crushed
$1/4$ tsp salt
300ml plain yogurt (whole or
   low-fat)
150g cucumber, diced
1 tsp dried mint
Olive oil for drizzling
   (optional)

Preparation time: 10 minutes

- Blend the crushed garlic and salt with the yogurt.

- Add the diced cucumber and combine with the yogurt.

- Sprinkle dried mint over the top and drizzle with a little oil, if using.

- This dish is always served with any lentil or rice dishes.

Cook's tip
- You can also use fresh mint when available and in season. When serving this salad as a dip, make sure you use the more set yogurt.

Tomato Salad

Salata Banadoura

This straightforward salad made with tomatoes, onions and fresh mint is an absolutely beautiful combination of flavours and takes just minutes to prepare. If you are like me, you'll always be happy to see it on the side of your plate.

SERVES 4

500g vine or cherry tomatoes
1 small red onion, cut in half and sliced
15g mint leaves, coarsely chopped
Juice of 1/2 lemon
30ml olive oil
1 clove garlic, crushed
1/2 tsp salt

Preparation time: 5 minutes

• Place the tomatoes, onion and mint in a bowl.

• To make a dressing, separately blend together the lemon juice, oil, garlic and salt.

• Add the dressing to the salad and mix well.

• Serve this salad with any lentil or rice dishes.

Green Lentil Salad

Salata Adas

There is no end to the choice of lentil dishes in Lebanon, especially among those on a low income; equally, lentils are enjoyed by almost every Lebanese person. This is so easy to make; also very tasty and satisfying.

SERVES 4

150g green lentils
2 cloves garlic, crushed
Juice of 1 lemon
70ml olive oil
100g cherry tomatoes, sliced
100g onion, chopped
30g chopped coriander
2 tbsp pomegranate molasses
  (optional)

Preparation time: 10 minutes
Cooking time: 35 minutes

- Cook the lentils in boiling water for about 35 minutes. It may take longer depending on the variety, but make sure you don't overcook them.

- Drain the lentils and allow to cool while preparing the other ingredients.

- Blend the garlic, lemon juice and oil, then add to the cooled lentils with the remaining ingredients apart from the molasses and mix well.

- Add the molasses, if using.

- I like to serve this salad on a bed of lettuce leaves.

Cook's tip
- Some people don't like coriander. In this recipe it is equally delicious to substitute parsley instead.

Artichoke Hearts filled with Salad

Salata Ardi Showki

Artichokes are eaten in so many different ways when in season. At that time, you can buy the fresh hearts to avoid the hard work of removing the leaves. Frozen hearts are perfect to use all year round.

SERVES 4

8 fresh or frozen artichoke
   hearts
Salt
2–3 cloves garlic, crushed
50ml lemon juice, plus juice
   of $^1/_2$ lemon for cooking
   artichokes
50ml olive oil
50g carrots, finely chopped
50g courgettes, finely
   chopped
65g peppers, deseeded and
   chopped
35g onion, chopped
25g chopped parsley

Preparation time: 15 minutes
Cooking time: 15–20
   minutes

• Cook the artichoke hearts in boiling water with a little salt and the juice of $^1/_2$ lemon for 15–20 minutes until well cooked. Lemon juice stops the hearts from turning brown.

• Blend the garlic, 50ml lemon juice, oil and $^1/_2$ teaspoon salt, then mix with the carrots, courgettes, peppers, onion and parsley.

• Fill each heart with the salad, then top with the remaining juice left in the bowl.

Cook's tip
• Artichokes go well with lemon, so I recommend preparing this salad at least half an hour before serving, to allow time for the juice to be absorbed. Make sure the hearts are well cooked by pricking them with a knife or fork, as some take longer to cook.

Butter Bean Salad

Salata Fasoulia

This is a lovely, refreshing and filling salad. I am a big fan of butter beans and always enjoy this dish, which takes minutes to prepare when you have already cooked the beans.

SERVES 4

2 cloves garlic, crushed
$^1/_2$ tsp salt
Juice of 1 lemon
40ml olive oil
60g chopped spring onions,
  including the green leaves,
  trimmed
200g cherry or vine tomatoes
400g cooked (200g dried)
  butter beans (page xi)
1 tsp dried mint, to garnish

Preparation time: 10 minutes

• To make the dressing, crush the garlic with salt and blend with the lemon juice and oil.

• Add the spring onions and tomatoes to the butter beans, then add the dressing and combine.

• Turn out onto a serving dish, and sprinkle with dried mint to garnish.

• Serve with a green salad or as part of a salad spread.

Cook's tip
• For a more intense flavour, it's always best to prepare salads with pulses an hour before serving so the juices can be absorbed.

CHAPTER 4

Side Dishes and Snacks

Aklaat Idafeyeh

You'll never find only one dish on a guest's table. The Lebanese enjoy a variety of dishes and there are always side dishes served with the main course, if not as starters. Meal times are never rushed because food is there to be appreciated and enjoyed; this is also a time to bring the family together and to catch up.

In this chapter, dishes can be served on the side, as a quick lunch or as part of the *maza*. I have given suggestions with each recipe of when best to serve.

All Lebanese tend to go over the top when guests are visiting, making a surplus amount of food. Extra food is never wasted because it's the kind that only improves in flavour over time. To this day, when they know I've had guests, my children hunt for leftovers in the fridge!

Aubergines with Tomatoes and Onions

Msaka'at Batingane

This very popular recipe is simpler than it looks, and you can never make too much of it because it is served cold. Kept in the fridge, it makes a delicious ready-made snack and can be served as part of a *maza*.

SERVES 4

100ml olive oil
400g (2 large) onions, cut in half and sliced
6 cloves garlic, peeled
800g aubergines, cut in half and sliced 2cm thick
3–4 red or green chillies, whole (optional)
500g tomatoes, cut into quarters
1 good tsp of salt

Preparation time: 10 minutes
Cooking time: 25 minutes

• Heat the oil and fry the onion and whole garlic cloves until golden brown.

• Add the aubergine slices and stir-fry with the onion and garlic for 5 minutes.

• Add the chillies, if using, and stir-fry for another minute.

• Add the tomatoes and salt; stir. Turn the heat to low, cover the pan and allow the aubergines to simmer in their own juice for 15–20 minutes, making sure most of the liquid has evaporated. Allow to cool before serving.

• Serve this dish cold with pitta bread, either as a side dish or a snack.

Spicy Potatoes with Fresh Coriander, Chilli and Garlic

Batata Harrah

I am not a big fan of potatoes but when *Batata Harrah* is served, I just can't resist it. When eating out in Lebanon, people often choose this as one of the starter dishes because, like me, everyone loves it. The Lebanese are not too tolerant of hot spicy food, however, and some prefer to have it without chilli; it still tastes good.

SERVES 4

100ml oil
750g potatoes, peeled and
    cut into cubes
4 large cloves garlic, finely
    chopped
2 green or red chillis
    (optional), deseeded and
    chopped
1 tsp salt
50g chopped fresh coriander

Preparation time: 10 minutes
Cooking time: 30 minutes

• Heat the oil and fry the potato cubes until they are golden brown.

• Add the garlic, chilli and salt and continue to fry for another minute.

• Lastly, add the coriander and gently turn to mix while still cooking for another two minutes.

• Serve this dish hot with wedges of lemon as a side dish or with *maza* (starters).

Bulgur Wheat Cooked with Tomatoes

Burghul Ma'A Banadoura

Many of the old-fashioned dishes have been forgotten except perhaps this one, often cooked as a main meal by people who live in the mountains. *Burghul M'a A Banadoura* is easy to prepare with ingredients that are in every kitchen. When there is nothing else available, this is always a good solution.

SERVES 4

70ml olive oil
250g (1 large) onion, chopped
500g ripe tomatoes, diced
1 tsp salt
1/2 tsp black pepper
300g *burghul* (bulgur wheat)

Preparation time: 10 minutes
Cooking time: 30 minutes

• Heat the oil and fry the onion until golden.

• Add the diced tomatoes, salt and ground black pepper. Cover the saucepan and simmer on low heat for about 5 minutes.

• Rinse the *burghul* and drain, then add to the tomatoes and onion.

• Cover and cook for another 15 minutes on low heat, allowing the *burghul* to cook in the tomato juice. If there isn't enough juice from the tomatoes, add a little water and cook until the water has evaporated.

• Serve with cabbage salad (page 62).

• This can be served as a main or a side dish.

Cook's tip
• Some people like to add some cooked chickpeas to this dish, but I was brought up having it without chickpeas.

Ado/Taro Roots with Garlic and Sumac Sauce

Kilkass Bsoumac

Kilkass (ado or taro root) is the loveliest root vegetable and commonly used and cultivated in Lebanon, mainly in winter. Often found in Asian and Middle Eastern stores, I was thrilled to find it in one of the big supermarkets recently. When I make this tasty dish, I literally hang around the kitchen until it's all gone. Worth a try.

SERVES 4

4 cloves garlic, crushed
4 tsp sumac
Juice of 1 juicy lemon
400ml warm water
1$^1/_2$ tsp salt
1kg *kilkass* (taro or ado root), peeled and cut into 3cm thick slices
Oil, for frying
Flour, for coating

Preparation time: 15 minutes
Cooking time: 30 minutes

• Prepare the sauce before cooking by simply mixing together the garlic, sumac, lemon juice, warm water and $^1/_2$ teaspoon salt.

• In boiling water with 1 teaspoon salt, boil the *kilkass* for about 10 minutes, until still slightly al dente, then drain.

• Heat the oil, toss the *kilkass* pieces in flour to coat and then fry them in batches until brown and crispy.

• Remove from the oil and drop the pieces in the sumac sauce. Repeat the same method with the remaining *kilkass*.

• Serve this unique combination as side dish or a snack, with nothing more than bread to enjoy its flavour.

Cook's tip

• *Kilkass* or *kilcas* is a seasonal root vegetable, which is found mostly in late autumn and winter.

Potato Cake

Kalib Batata

We all understand the importance of food presentation, often eating what pleases the eye. This potato dish tastes as good as it looks. You may add other vegetables to the filling to turn it into a meal on its own.

SERVES 4–6

1kg potatoes
100ml olive oil
600g (3 large) onions, sliced
3–4 tsp sumac
1½ tsp salt
50g butter
100g crème fraîche
3 egg yolks
2 tbsp breadcrumbs

Preparation time: 15 minutes
Cooking time: 20 minutes,
  plus 35 minutes' baking

• Peel and cut the potatoes into chunks, then cook in boiling water for 20 minutes until they are soft enough for mashing.

• Preheat the oven to 200°C/400°F/gas mark 6.

• Meanwhile, heat the oil and fry the onion slices until soft and golden brown, then add the sumac, and ½ teaspoon salt and stir for 1 minute.

• Drain the potatoes and mash to a creamy consistency, then stir in the butter, crème fraîche, 1 teaspoon salt and two of the egg yolks and combine well.

• Divide the mashed potatoes in half and smoothly spread one half over the base of a greased oven dish, about 25cm in diameter.

• Spread the onions evenly on top, then top with the remaining potatoes and smooth the surface.

• Beat the remaining egg yolk and brush on top, then sprinkle with breadcrumbs.

• Bake in the preheated oven for 30 minutes until the surface is crisp and golden.

• Serve this dish with any other vegetable dish or on its own with a mixed salad.

Dill/Parsley Omelette

Iget Shoumar/Backdoonis

This omelette is the most common of Lebanese omelettes. It's usually made with parsley but sometimes with dill when in season. When I happen to be in the village in springtime, we head to the remote countryside to pick dill, sometimes taking bread, eggs and other ingredients with us to make omelettes with wild dill for our picnic. The sort of activity we loved as children, is now an occasional treat.

SERVES 4

6 large eggs
50g chopped fresh dill or
  parsley
30g white flour
160g (1 medium) onion,
  chopped
1 tsp cinnamon
½ tsp ground black pepper
1 tsp salt
50ml olive oil

Preparation time: 5 minutes
Cooking time: 10 minutes

• Whisk the eggs then add the remaining ingredients, *except* the oil, and mix well.

• Heat the oil in a frying pan and pour in the egg mixture (this can be done in smaller batches).

• Turn the heat to low and allow the omelette to cook for 5 minutes.

• Either turn the omelette over to brown on the other side or place it under a preheated grill.

• Serve with salad or just bread, either for a quick meal or a snack.

Cook's tip
• It is more common to make this recipe with parsley, as dill is not always available. Follow the same method for either.

Courgette Omelette

Iget Coosa

This is a great recipe that you can either enjoy as a snack or as a meal served with salad. I always like this sort of food wrapped in bread. It can also be made in small, individual portions.

SERVES 4

6 large eggs
1 tsp cinnamon
$^1/_2$–1 tsp salt
$^1/_2$ tsp ground black pepper
190g (1 medium) courgette, grated
70g (1 small) onion, chopped
50g tomatoes, chopped
100ml olive oil

Preparation time: 10 minutes
Cooking time: 10–15 minutes

- Whisk the eggs with the cinnamon, salt and pepper.

- Add the grated courgette and onion and combine, then stir in the tomatoes.

- Heat the oil in a frying pan and add the egg mixture. Turn the heat to low and allow to cook for 10 minutes.

- Finally, brown the top under the grill.

- Serve with bread and salad either as a main course or a light meal.

Cook's tip
- For a delicious snack, make small crispy omelettes instead of one large one.

Lemon Potatoes with Peppers

Batata Bhamoud

This is a great way to serve potatoes with just about anything. The dish's colourful presentation tells a lot about the many flavours it offers.

SERVES 4

100ml oil
800g potatoes, peeled and
  cut into 3cm cubes
1/2 red pepper, deseeded and
  chopped
1/2 green pepper, deseeded
  and chopped
1/2 yellow pepper, deseeded
  and chopped
2 medium onions, sliced into
  rings
6 whole cloves garlic, peeled
1 tsp salt
Juice of 1 lemon

Preparation time: 10 minutes
Cooking time: 35 minutes

• Heat some of the oil and fry the potatoes on a gentle heat until they are almost cooked through. Remove the potatoes from the pan and set aside.

• With the remaining oil, fry the peppers, onions and garlic to soften for about 10 minutes. Stir in the salt.

• Return the potatoes to the pan and cook for a further 5 minutes with the vegetables, making sure the potatoes are well-cooked in the centre.

• Stir in the lemon juice.

• Serve this dish hot with lemon wedges as a side dish or with *maza* (starters).

Cook's tip
• The garlic clove should still be whole when you finish cooking, so be careful when stirring and avoid stirring the ingredients too often.

Broad Beans with Coriander and Garlic

Foul Akhdar Be Couzbara

In my opinion, broad beans are so underestimated. When they are in season, the Lebanese buy many kilos a day, either for cooking or snacking on. Often, when visiting, a massive basket of broad beans is placed on the table for podding and eating while chatting. In this dish we use the pods as well as the beans – once you've tried it, you'll never throw the pods away again.

SERVES 4

1kg fresh tender broad beans
  in their pods
100ml olive oil
350g onions (about 2 large
  onions), chopped
4 plump cloves garlic,
  peeled and sliced
1 tsp salt
50g chopped coriander
2 lemons, cut into wedges

Preparation time: 20 minutes
Cooking time: 50 minutes

• Cut the ends off the beans, pull off any strings and cut into pieces about 4cm long. Rinse and drain.

• Heat 70ml of the oil and brown the onions and garlic.

• Add all the beans to the pan to fry with the onions, turn the heat down, cover and simmer for about 25 minutes, turning occasionally.

• When the beans are tender, uncover, add salt and allow to cook for a little longer, until they are well cooked and look sautéed. If in doubt, taste the beans.

• Reserving a little coriander for the garnish, add the rest to the broad beans and cook for 1–2 minutes. Turn off the heat and add the remaining oil.

• Serve this dish as a side dish or as a light meal with flat bread and lemon wedges.

• A bowl of plain yogurt on the side also goes well with this dish.

Cook's tip
• It is important to make sure that you prepare this dish with young, tender broad beans; they can become tough late season.

Fried Aubergines with Tomato Sauce

Batinagane Mekli Ma Banadoura

Bursting with flavours, this dish is a must-try. When a Lebanese person says they are having a 'mixed fry-up', it means fried aubergines, onions, courgettes and potatoes, and it's always served with tomato sauce.

SERVES 4

2 large aubergines
Salt
50ml olive oil
3 cloves garlic, crushed
1 or 2 chillies (optional), deseeded and chopped or whole
400g fresh tomatoes, chopped
A little chopped parsley, to garnish
Cooking oil, for frying

Preparation time: 10 minutes, plus 1 hour to salt aubergines
Cooking time: 30–40 minutes

• Slice the aubergines into 1cm thick pieces. Sprinkle with plenty of salt and leave in a colander to drain for 1 hour (salting aubergines reduces the amount of oil they absorb).

• Heat a little cooking oil in a frying pan and fry the aubergines to brown on both sides. Or, if you want to avoid frying, use a griddle, brushing the aubergines with oil, and brown them on both sides.

• To make a tomato sauce, heat the olive oil, add garlic and chilli and stir for 30 seconds; do not allow the garlic to turn brown.

• Add the tomatoes and fry with the chilli and garlic for 5 minutes.

• Either serve the tomato sauce on the side or spooned over the aubergines.

• Allow to cool and sprinkle with chopped parsley.

• Serve cold with bread.

Cook's tip
• I am passionate about aubergines, so I like to enjoy this dish on its own just with bread. It can also be served as a side dish with a main course.

Pumpkin and Bulgur Wheat Balls
Kebbeh Lakteen

Kebbeh is the Lebanese national dish. It is mostly made with meat, fish, potatoes or pumpkin. This is the vegetarian *kebbeh*, which is equally popular among non-vegetarians. The *kebbeh* balls are served with *maza* (starters), as snacks or as a side dish.

MAKES ABOUT 15 BALLS

1 x ½ quantity of *kebbeh* dough (page 164)
1 x ½ quantity of *kebbeh* filling (page 164)
Cooking oil, for deep-frying

Preparation time: 1 hour
Cooking time: 30–40 minutes

• Using the same method as page 164, make up the *kebbeh* dough and filling.

• Take a piece of *kebbeh* dough and roll it between the palms of your hands to make a ball of golf-ball size.

• Make a hollow space in the middle, fill with 1 teaspoon of the filling and seal the end. Make sure it is smooth all the way round, without any cracks. Repeat with the remaining dough and filling.

• Make the filled balls into a longer shape, similar to a rugby ball. (Follow steps as in photos.)

• Heat the oil and deep-fry the *kebbeh* balls on a medium heat, making sure they are separated and do not stick together.

• When the *kebbeh* balls are brown (about 10 minutes), remove from the oil and place them on kitchen towels to absorb any excess oil.

• Serve hot on their own or with salad.

Cook's tip
• You can make these bite sized and serve with canapés at parties or with a buffet spread.

Smoked Aubergine with Yogurt

Fetteh Batingane

Fetteh is made with various ingredients. This aubergine *fetteh* can be created with either fried or smoked aubergines. Try both and see which you prefer.

SERVES 4

500g (1 large) aubergine
150g toasted pitta bread
A little oil, for drizzling the bread
350g natural yogurt
2 cloves garlic, crushed
1 tsp salt
A little dried mint, for sprinkling

Preparation time: 10 minutes
Cooking time: 20 minutes

• For a smoky flavour, place the aubergine on the flame of a gas hob, turning every few minutes, for about 20 minutes until the centre is tender. Remove from the flame and allow to cool enough to handle. If frying, cut into 3cm cubes and brown.

• If smoked, remove the skin, then rinse under a cold tap to remove any remaining pieces of skin.

• Break the pitta bread into small pieces, spread out on a baking tray and drizzle with a little oil. Toast either in the oven at 200°C/400°F/gas mark 6 or under the grill.

• Reserving a few pieces to garnish the surface, place the rest of the toasted bread in the bottom of a serving bowl.

• Cut the aubergine into bite-sized pieces and spread over the toasted bread.

• Mix the yogurt with the garlic and salt then pour over the aubergines.

• Garnish with the remaining toast and sprinkle with a little dried mint.

• Serve at once either as a light lunch or as a starter.

Cook's tip
• You may set *fetteh* in individual serving dishes.

Chickpeas with Garlic Yogurt

Fetteh Hummus

Breakfast cafés are a special feature throughout cities in Lebanon and they are not for dainty eaters. These places are usually packed with early workers dosing themselves up with high-energy, completely vegetarian food at very low cost. The dishes, based only on a mixed plate of *hummus, balila, foul mdammas and fetteh hummus*, are prepared on a counter in front of you – you just pull up a chair and wait only ten minutes for your food. A real treat!

SERVES 4

150g Lebanese or pitta bread
2 tbsp oil
15g pine nuts (optional)
250g (125g dried) hot
   cooked chickpeas (page xi)
2 small cloves garlic,
   crushed
¹/₂ tsp salt
400g plain yogurt
Good pinch of ground cumin

Preparation time: 10–15
   minutes, plus soaking
   overnight
Cooking time: 1 hour, to
   cook chickpeas

• Split and cut the bread into small pieces, place on a baking tray, drizzle with little oil and brown in the oven at 200°C/400°F/gas mark 6 or under the grill.

• Heat the remaining oil and fry the pine nuts, if using, to brown. Place on kitchen paper to absorb the oil.

• Place the toasted bread in the bottom of a serving bowl, then spread the chickpeas on top (the chickpeas must be hot), reserving a few for garnish.

• Blend crushed garlic and salt with the yogurt and pour over the chickpeas.

• Sprinkle the pine nuts and cumin over the top.

• Serve at once either for breakfast or early lunch. It can also be served with *maza* (starters) at the beginning of a meal.

Cook's tip
• When you have to use tinned chickpeas, it is a good idea to boil them for a few minutes in fresh water to reduce the 'tinny' taste.

Roasted Cauliflower

Karnabeet Meshwi

Cauliflower is usually fried in Lebanese cooking, but like many people I avoid fried food so prefer to roast it instead. This very simple recipe will impress whoever you serve it to. It's my nine-year-old grandson's favourite. He calls it 'burnt cauliflower' and this is what we all call it now.

SERVES 4

1 medium cauliflower,
  broken into florets
1 tsp salt
2 tbsp olive oil
Lemon wedges, to serve

Preparation time: 5 minutes
Cooking time: 50–55
  minutes

• Preheat the oven to 220°C/425°F/gas mark 7.

• Rinse the florets in cold water and place on a baking tray while still very wet.

• Sprinkle with salt and drizzle with oil, then turn the florets to coat.

• Bake in the preheated oven for 50–55 minutes. Allow few more minutes if needed, to make sure the florets are brown and a little crispy on the surface.

• Serve as a side dish with bread, lemon wedges and tahini sauce (page 266). It can also be served as a starter, picked up with a piece of bread, then dipped in the tahini sauce.

Cook's tip
• It is important to serve this dish with tahini sauce as the flavours complement each other well.

Warm Chickpeas with Lemon Dressing

Balila

Tasty and economical, this dish shows the Lebanese love for chickpeas, even when prepared in the simplest way.

SERVES 4

Juice of 1 lemon
2 cloves garlic, crushed
$\frac{1}{2}$ tsp salt
300g well-cooked (150g dried) chickpeas (page xi)
2 tbsp olive oil
$\frac{1}{2}$ tsp ground cumin

Preparation time: 10 minutes, plus soaking overnight
Cooking time: 1 hour, to cook chickpeas

• To make the dressing, combine the lemon juice, garlic and salt.

• If not hot, heat the chickpeas, drain and place in a serving bowl.

• Add the dressing and mix well.

• Pour the olive oil over the top and sprinkle with the cumin.

• Serve hot with bread as a starter, breakfast or a side dish.

Cook's tip
• I love indulging in this dish for late breakfast. Delicious and easy to digest, it sets me up for the day.

Minty Grated Courgettes
Coosa Mtabbal

The Lebanese don't like to waste food; whenever they make stuffed courgettes they save the insides for this recipe. It is just as good made with grated courgettes at any time.

SERVES 4

50ml olive oil, plus a little
　for drizzling
200g (1 large) onion, finely
　diced
600g courgettes, coarsely
　grated
50ml lemon juice (1 juicy
　lemon)
3 cloves garlic, crushed
1 tsp salt
1 tsp dried mint, with a little
　extra for sprinkling

Preparation time: 10 minutes
Cooking time: 20–25
　minutes

• Heat the oil and fry the onion until golden brown.

• Add the grated courgettes and stir-fry with the onion to soften.

• When the moisture has evaporated, add the lemon juice, garlic, salt and mint. Stir and cook for another minute or two.

• Turn out onto a serving plate, drizzle with little oil and sprinkle with dried mint.

• Serve warm with lemon wedges and toasted pitta bread as a snack or side dish.

Scrambled Eggs with Potatoes and Garlic
Mfaraket Batata Wa Bayd

When you look at this recipe you'll think there isn't much to it, but believe me, as soon as you make it, you'll want to eat it immediately. I used to watch my uncle having it for breakfast, skipping the potatoes and adding twice the amount of garlic, saying it gave him energy all day.

SERVES 4

60ml oil
600g potatoes, peeled and
    cut into small cubes
8 cloves garlic, peeled and
    cut in half
6 eggs
1 tsp salt
1/2 tsp black pepper
1 tsp ground cinnamon

Preparation time: 15 minutes
Cooking time: 20 minutes

• Heat the oil and fry the potato cubes until they are slightly brown.

• Add the garlic halves and fry with the potatoes for few minutes, making sure they don't turn brown.

• Cover and cook for a few minutes until everything is softened, before turning off the heat.

• Add the eggs and turn with the potatoes. Cook for 5 minutes until the eggs are cooked.

• Add salt and pepper and sprinkle cinnamon over the top.

• Serve with bread and salad as a quick meal or a snack.

Dried Broad Beans in Lemon Dressing

Foul Mdammas

This is classed as fast food, you just step into a *foul* café for breakfast and it's ready in minutes. At home we have it as brunch. It is always scooped with bread and must be served with condiments such as mint, radishes, onions, tomatoes and pickles.

SERVES 4

250g dried broad beans
   (500g cooked), or 2 tins
   (480g drained)
Juice of 1 lemon
2 cloves garlic, crushed
1 tsp salt
2 tbsp olive oil

Preparation time: 10 minutes
Cooking time: 1 hour, if
   using dried beans

• If using dried beans, soak overnight then boil in plain water for about an hour until the beans are very tender.

• Remove from the water, reserving a little for adding later if the beans are dry, then lightly squash with a fork.

• Add lemon juice, garlic and salt and mix with the beans. Add a little of the reserved stock for moisture if needed.

• Divide into serving portions and drizzle generously with olive oil.

• Serve with pitta bread and condiments, such as mint, tomatoes and sliced onion. This dish always makes a great snack or a quick meal.

Egg with Chilli Tomatoes

Bayd Ma Banadoura

This country dish is usually made for breakfast but for me it makes the perfect snack anytime. It is quick to prepare and tastier than you might expect.

SERVES 4

40ml olive oil
120g (1 medium) onion, finely chopped
500g tomatoes, chopped
1 red chilli, deseeded and chopped, or 1 tsp chilli powder (optional)
6 eggs
1 tsp salt
Ground black pepper

Preparation time: 5–10 minutes
Cooking time: 15 minutes

• Heat the oil in a frying pan and fry the onion until it begins to brown.

• Add the tomatoes and chilli to the onion and cook for a few minutes.

• Crack the eggs onto the tomatoes, add the salt and turn the mixture to scramble. Cook for few minutes until all the eggs are set with no runny bits. Sprinkle with black pepper.

• Serve hot with bread.

Potato with Bulgur Wheat and Walnuts

Kebbeh Batata

As I mentioned in the other *kebbeh* recipes, this is a national dish. There are many versions and here is another, which is so quick to make and quite delicious.

SERVES 4

800g potatoes
100g chopped walnuts
60g *burghul* (bulgur wheat), rinsed and drained
135g onion, grated
½ tsp mixed spices (page 258)
1 tsp salt
10g chopped mint, plus a few leaves for garnish
10g chopped basil leaves
50ml olive oil (use less if you prefer)
3 or 4 walnut halves, for garnish
1 tsp sumac to sprinkle on top (optional)

Preparation time: 15 minutes
Cooking time: 20–25 minutes

- Peel the potatoes and cook in boiling water for about 20–25 minutes until tender.

- Process the walnuts in a blender or food processor until they resemble breadcrumbs.

- Mash the potatoes and mix in the remaining ingredients, except for the oil, walnut halves and sumac.

- Turn the mixture out onto a serving plate, roughing the surface with the back of a spoon.

- Decorate with walnut halves and few mint leaves and drizzle with oil. Sprinkle with sumac, if using.

- Serve with mint on the side.

Cook's tip
- I sometimes serve this as a meal with a simple salad of tomato and coarsly chopped mint leaves as well as with *maza* (starters).

CHAPTER 5

Bread and Savoury Pastries
Khibez Wa Maajanat

The main source of carbohydrate in Lebanon, bread is always served with meals. There are a few types of bread and they are all flat, which is perfect for the way we eat. Food is picked up with small pieces of bread and with some dishes it doesn't feel right to use a fork.

Savoury pastries (*maajanat*) are mostly made with bread dough and no fat is required. Because of their popularity, *maajanat* are served at home, in restaurants, or bought from bakeries ready to eat on the move. *Maajanat* are extremely popular, especially the spinach triangles; they always make a great addition to the table when served at dinner parties.

I have also included some *manoushi* recipes in this chapter. *Manoushi* is real street food that you buy and eat on the go, from morning till midday. *Manoushi* bakeries are normally shut by lunchtime.

Spinach Triangles

Fatayer Sabanekh

Spinach triangles are by far the most popular pastries. They are served on every occasion as well as being bought from bakeries to eat as a snack. Spinach with onions and sumac gives a wonderful flavour and makes a great combination.

MAKES 15, DEPENDING ON THE SIZE

For the dough
Use the same ingredients and method as for *Fatayer Hummus* (page 132)

For the filling
200g spinach, chopped
30ml olive oil, plus extra for brushing
150g (1 medium) onion, chopped
Juice of 1 lemon
1 heaped tsp sumac
1 level tsp salt

Preparation time: 1 hour, plus dough rising time
Cooking time: 15 minutes

• Prepare the dough (page 132), leaving it to double in size (around 2 hours).

• Preheat the oven to 240°C/475°F/gas mark 9.

• Mix the spinach with the remaining filling ingredients and set aside while rolling the dough.

• Knead the dough and roll out thinly onto a floured surface. Cut out circles about 10cm in diameter with a round cutter using all the dough (gather the trimmings together and re-roll).

• Squeeze out the juice from the spinach and place a heaped teaspoonful of the filling in the centre of each circle. Fold two sides of the dough to the middle of the circle and squeeze the edges to stick together, then fold the third side to join in the middle and stick the sides together by squeezing firmly (see step photos).

• Place the triangles on a heated, greased baking tray, with a little space between them as they will expand. Brush lightly with oil.

• Bake in the preheated oven for 10–15 minutes until lightly browned.

• Serve hot or cold.

Cook's tip
• It may seem strange to bake the triangles on such a high heat, but they need to be cooked quickly otherwise the dough will become hard. They freeze well before baking for up to 4 months and can be cooked straight from the freezer.

Courgette and Onion Filled Triangles

Fatayer Coosa

This is another traditional recipe. It is very popular among country people, who sometimes use pumpkin instead of courgettes, but the remaining ingredients are the same apart from the coriander.

MAKES 12–15 TRIANGLES

For the dough
Use the same ingredients
   and method as for *Fatayer
   Hummus* (page 132)

For the filling
300g courgettes, diced
1 tsp salt
50ml olive oil, plus extra for
   brushing
100g (1 small–medium)
   onion, chopped
1 tomato, chopped
2 cloves garlic, chopped
20g chopped fresh coriander
1 tsp ground cinnamon
1 tsp mixed spices (page
   258)

Preparation time: 40–50
   minutes, plus dough rising
   time
Cooking time: 15–20
   minutes

• Place the courgettes in a colander, add the salt and leave for 30 minutes to drain a little.

• For the filling, combine the courgettes with all the remaining filling ingredients and set aside while preparing and rolling out the dough.

• Preheat the oven to 240°C/475°F/gas mark 9.

• Knead the dough and roll out thinly onto a floured surface. Cut out circles about 10cm diameter with a round cutter using all the dough (gather the trimmings together and re-roll).

• Spoon 1 dessertspoon of filling into the centre of each circle. Fold two sides of the dough to the middle of the circle and squeeze the edges to stick together, then fold the third side to join in the middle and stick the sides together by squeezing firmly (see photos).

• Place on a greased, heated baking tray, leaving a little space between them, and lightly brush each triangle with a little oil. Bake in the preheated oven for 15–20 minutes until the pastries are lightly browned.

• Serve hot or cold.

Cook's tip
• You can freeze these before cooking and bake straight from the freezer.

Chickpea Pasties

Fatayer Hummus

I rediscovered this traditional recipe while visiting a bakery. When I discussed it with people in the village, they all seemed surprised and were reminded of a long-forgotten, delicious recipe.

MAKES ABOUT 15

For the dough
400g plain flour, wholemeal or mixed, plus a little for rolling out
2 tsp instant dried yeast
1/2 tsp salt
2 tbsp oil
Lukewarm water

For the filling
150g dried chickpeas, soaked overnight
50ml olive oil
150g (I medium) onion, chopped
30g chopped coriander
1 tsp ground cumin
1 tsp cinnamon
1/2 tsp salt

Preparation time: 30–40 minutes, plus up to 2 hours for dough to rise
Cooking time: 20 minutes, plus 15 minutes' baking

Cook's tip
• You must always use dried and soaked chickpeas for this recipe, never cooked. The pasties can be frozen before baking for up to 4 months.

• Mix together the flour, yeast and salt. Add the oil and gradually add just enough water to make a smooth dough. Knead thoroughly for a few minutes.

• Place the dough in a bowl at least twice its size, cover with a damp tea towel and leave in a warm place until it doubles in size. (May take around 2 hours.)

• Preheat the oven to 240°C/475°F/gas mark 9.

• To make the filling, drain the chickpeas and process in a food processor until the mixture resembles breadcrumbs in texture.

• Heat the oil in a frying pan and fry the onion to brown. Add the minced chickpeas, coriander and the spices. Cook for 5 minutes, then add the salt.

• When the dough is doubled in size, remove it from the bowl and roll into a ball to squeeze out the air.

• On a floured surface, roll out the dough thinly and cut circles with a round cutter, 10–12cm in diameter.

• Spoon 1 dessertspoon of filling onto each circle, fold over the dough and firmly stick the edges together, then score with a fork to seal, as shown in the photos.

• Place the crescents on a heated, oiled baking tray and lightly brush each one with little oil. Bake in the preheated oven for 15 minutes until the pastries are lightly browned.

• *Fatayer hummus* are excellent to have in the house for healthy snacks.

Lebanese Bread

Khibez

Bread must always be present on any dinner table in Lebanon. You tear and share, dipping and scooping food. Many people never use a fork but take every mouthful with a piece of bread. It is easy enough to make, though a little time-consuming.

MAKES ABOUT 15

500g strong bread flour, wholemeal or mixed, plus extra for rolling out
1 sachet instant dried yeast (7g)
1 tsp salt
Lukewarm water

Preparation time: 40 minutes, plus dough rising time
Cooking time: 15 minutes each batch

• Mix the flour with the yeast and salt, then gradually add enough water to create a smooth, non-sticky dough. Knead the dough until it becomes smooth without any pockets of flour.

• Place the dough in a bowl, making sure it is big enough for the dough to double in size. Cover with a damp tea towel and keep in a warm place for about 2 hours until doubled in size.

• Preheat the oven to 240°C/475°F/gas mark 9 and place a flat baking tray inside to heat.

• Knead the dough again and divide it into small balls slightly smaller than tennis balls.

• Roll each one on a floured surface into a flat circle about ¹/₂cm thick. When you have finished rolling them out, leave to rest for a few minutes.

• Now begin baking by placing the dough circles a few at the time on the heated baking tray, leaving space between them to allow for rising. Bake for 15 minutes.

• After a few minutes, the heat will rise to the top part of the dough, making each loaf split into two layers before it turns slightly golden.

• The bread is now puffed up by the hot air between the two layers, so take care if you break into it while still very hot.

Cook's tip
• I make a large batch of bread, pile it up when cooled and push the air out so I can freeze it without taking up too much space in the freezer. When Lebanese bread is not available, serve pitta bread with your meals.

Cheese Crescents

Sambousak Jibneh

Sambousak is always served at parties along with other pastries. Suitable for buffets, snacks and canapés, it is often served as part of a *maza* spread. For such events they are made bite-sized.

MAKES 12–15

30ml oil, plus extra for frying
Pinch of salt
220g plain flour, plus extra
  for rolling out
Lukewarm water
200g feta cheese
100g (1 small) red onion,
  chopped
25g chopped flat parsley

Preparation time: 30–40
  minutes, plus 30 minutes
  for pastry to rest
Cooking time: 15–20
  minutes

• To make the pastry, rub 30ml oil and a pinch of salt into the flour until it becomes a little crumbly. Adding a little water at a time, continue to rub until the mixture forms a smooth, non-sticky pastry.

• Wrap with clingfilm (plastic wrap) and leave to rest in the fridge for 30 minutes.

• Crumble the cheese with the tips of your fingers then mix in the onion and parsley (no salt is needed as feta cheese is usually salty).

• Roll the pastry onto a lightly floured surface and cut into 8cm circles.

• Place 1 teaspoon of the filling in the centre of each circle, fold over and squeeze the edges firmly together to close. Starting from one corner, pinch and twist the edges all the way round to the other corner to create a decorative edge.

• Heat the oil in a frying pan and fry the *sambousak* over medium heat to brown on both sides.

• Serve warm.

Cook's tip
• You may bake the *sambousak* if you prefer to avoid frying. Bake in an oven preheated to 220°C/425°F/gas mark 7 for 10–15 minutes.

Egg Pizza
Manoushi Bayd

When visiting Furn Al Sabaya, I learnt how to make one of their speciality *manoushi* (pizza). The sisters who own and run this modest little bakery were so accommodating when I asked if I could take pictures step by step while they were working, and were more than happy to give me their recipes.

MAKES 2

200g plain flour, plus extra
  for rolling out
2 tsp dried instant yeast
Pinch of salt
Lukewarm water
4 large eggs
10g chopped fresh mint
Salt to taste
Ground black pepper
Olive oil

Preparation time: 15
  minutes, plus extra for
  dough rising time
Cooking time: 20 minutes

• Make the dough by mixing together the flour, yeast and salt, adding a little water at a time to form a non-sticky dough; knead for few minutes. Rest the dough for an hour until it doubles in size.

• Preheat the oven to 240°C/475°F/gas mark 9.

• Divide the dough into two balls and roll each ball out onto a floured surface into $^{1}/_{2}$cm thick circles.

• Place the flat dough on a heated baking tray and bake a for few minutes in the preheated oven. Remove from the oven while the dough is still soft and the top layer has just begun to rise.

• Make a barrier to retain the eggs by shaping the edge of the loaves upwards all the way round, then peel off the top layer of the loaf (this layer is not used again once removed).

• Crack 2 eggs into the centre of each loaf, add the mint, salt, pepper and a drizzle of olive oil, then gently whisk with fork. Return to the oven and bake for about 15 minutes until the eggs are set.

• Serve with few slices of tomatoes on the side, extra mint and some olives.

Thyme and Cheese Lebanese Pizza

Manoushi

A *manoushi* comes with a number of toppings, mainly *za'atar* (wild thyme) or cheese, plus non-vegetarian varieties. The most popular food to eat on the go, in busy areas you will find a *manoushi* bakery every 100 metres or so and they are all busy. At home, *manoushis* are made or brought in from the bakery for weekend breakfasts when all the family gather together.

MAKES 8–10

For the dough
500g strong bread flour, plus
   extra for rolling out
1 sachet instant yeast (7g)
1 tsp salt

For the toppings
10g *za'atar* (thyme)
10g sesame seeds
5g sumac
$\frac{1}{2}$ tsp salt
60ml olive oil
500g halloumi or feta
   cheese, grated

Preparation time: 30 minutes
Cooking time: 1 hour

• Make the dough following the same method as for Lebanese Bread (page 134).

• Mix together the *za'atar* and all the other topping ingredients, except for the cheese.

• When the dough is ready, roll it out onto a floured surface and divide into 8–10 balls.

• Roll the balls into circles about $\frac{1}{2}$cm thick and make dents on the surface with your fingertips to prevent the dough from splitting and filling with air.

• Spread half of the loaves with *za'atar* mix and the other half with the grated cheese.

• Place a few *manoushis* at a time on a heated baking tray and bake in a preheated oven at 240°C/475°F/gas mark 9 for 10–15 minutes. *Manoushis* will cook more quickly if using an electric oven, so keep an eye on them so they don't overcook.

• Serve warm.

Cook's tip
• Miniature *manoushis* are often served as part of a buffet or as canapés. It is quite an effort to prepare *manoushis*, so I tend to make them when the family are around, as it's fun to enjoy them as a group.

CHAPTER 6
Main Dishes
Wajbat Ra'eesiyeh

An endless variety of home-cooked Lebanese dishes can be served as a main course. When I started writing this book, I aimed for a certain number of recipes but it got a bit out of control once I'd started! I never imagined it would be easy to find so many vegetarian main dishes, all too good to leave out. Finally, I had to limit the number and stop.

Stews are the most frequently cooked main meals, both vegetarian and non-vegetarian, and always served with Lebanese rice (page 264). This version is cooked with vermicelli pasta, which adds a special flavour to the rice. Most Lebanese will only have rice cooked with vermicelli.

In this chapter, you'll find stews, rice dishes, baked vegetables and more variations of the Lebanese national dish, *kebbeh*. There are also dishes made with *burghul* (bulgur wheat), which is sometimes served as an alternative to rice.

The author and her son, Neil, cooking falafel

Mixed Pulse and Herb Patties
Falafel

Falafel is the most popular street food in all Middle Eastern countries. People rarely make falafel at home because there are falafel shops on almost every street in every city open from morning to late night. Nutritious, flavoursome and very economical, everyone can afford to buy a falafel wrap. However, they are easy to make and if dried broad beans are unavailable, they can be made using only chickpeas.

SERVES 4–6

150g dried chickpeas
150g skinless, dried broad beans (if unavailable substitute with chickpeas)
1 medium onion, coarsely chopped
5 cloves garlic, peeled
30g fresh coriander
20g fresh parsley
50g ground coriander seeds
1 tsp salt
1 tsp ground black pepper
2 tsp baking powder
Oil, for frying

Preparation time: 40 minutes, plus soaking overnight
Cooking time: 30 minutes

• Soak the chickpeas and broad beans overnight.

• Drain the chickpeas and broad beans and finely mince in a food processor. Add the onion, garlic and all the herbs, coriander seeds, salt and pepper and process all together to form a dough.

• It is always better to allow the falafel mixture to absorb the flavours for a few hours before frying.

• When you are ready to start cooking, add the baking powder to the mixture. Roll pieces of dough into little balls slightly pressed between the palms of your hands to form small patties.

• Heat the oil and deep-fry the falafel for about 10 minutes over a medium heat until they turn brown and are cooked in the middle.

• Falafel is always served with pickled turnips, tomatoes and chopped parsley and drizzled with Tahini Sauce (page 266). You will also need either Lebanese Bread (page 134) or pitta bread to make the wrap.

Cook's tip
• Falafel mix freezes well for up to 6 months if you prefer to make a large batch, but don't add the baking powder until it is defrosted and you are about to start cooking.

Lentils with Pasta

Roushta

This is a traditional recipe that has made a comeback. In the past, many Lebanese people would have said they'd never heard of it unless they grew up in the mountains, but now they are familiar with this very tasty dish, which requires only a few ingredients.

SERVES 4

250g green or brown lentils
1.5ltr boiling water
120g plain flour, plus extra
  for rolling out
Salt
Lukewarm water
70ml olive oil
250g (2 medium) onions,
  chopped
4 cloves garlic, crushed
40g chopped coriander
  leaves

Preparation time: 20–25
  minutes
Cooking time: 1 hour

• Cook the lentils in the boiling water for about 40 minutes on a low heat, making sure they are well cooked.

• At the same time, prepare the pasta by mixing the flour with a pinch of salt and adding little water at a time until you have a smooth dough. Set aside to rest until needed.

• Heat two thirds of the oil and fry the onions to brown, then add to the lentils with 1 teaspoon of salt and continue cooking.

• Thinly roll the dough out onto a floured surface and cut into strips measuring about 2 x 7cm. Drop them separately into the lentils and continue cooking for another 10 minutes.

• Reserving a little coriander for the garnish, heat the remaining oil and fry the garlic and coriander for a few seconds.

• Add the garlic and coriander to the lentils and cook for another minute or two.

• Garnish with reserved coriander and serve hot or cold with salad.

Cook's tip
• Avoid stirring the *roushta* too often after adding the pasta to the lentils, as this can make them stick together.

Stuffed Cabbage Leaves

Mehshi Malfoof

In the Middle East you will find a variety of stuffed vegetables, mostly made with the same filling, everything from potatoes to vine leaves, to aubergines and courgettes. For this recipe you'll need the more tender leaves of a cabbage such as Sweetheart or January King.

SERVES 4

550g trimmed cabbage
   leaves, middle stalks
   trimmed off and reserved

For the filling
300g Italian risotto or
   pudding rice, rinsed and
   soaked for 1/2 to 1 hour
100g chopped flat parsley
25g chopped mint leaves
180g spring onions, trimmed
   and chopped
500g tomatoes, chopped
Juice of 1 lemon
1 tsp salt
50ml olive oil
5 or 6 cherry tomatoes

For the sauce
500ml hot water
Juice of 1 lemon
1 tbsp olive oil
1/2 tsp salt

Preparation time: 40 minutes
Cooking time: 50 minutes

• Blanch the cabbage leaves and stalks in boiling water for a few minutes to soften and then drain through a sieve.

• Drain the rice, add to the remaining filling ingredients apart from the cherry tomatoes and mix well.

• Halve the cabbage leaves if too big and flatten on a smooth surface. Place 1 or 2 teaspoons of the filling horizontally along the centre, fold the top end of the leaf over the filling and roll it firmly to the end (see photos).

• Line the bottom of a saucepan with the middle stalks you trimmed off and place the cabbage rolls evenly on top, allowing enough space in the pot, as the rice will swell. Place the cherry tomatoes on top.

• Combine all the sauce ingredients and pour over the cabbage. Bring to the boil, then cover the pot. Reduce the heat to medium–low and cook for 1 hour.

• Take one roll out to test. If the rice is not ready, cook for few more minutes before turning out onto a serving dish.

• Serve cold with bread and lemon wedges. Cabbage and lemon always go well together.

Cook's tip
• You can prepare this dish in advance, but add the sauce only when you begin to cook.

Chickpeas with Bulgur Wheat

Burghul Bidfeen

There are so many dishes we love but don't get around to making. This peasant dish, made with only a few basic ingredients, is very popular in the mountains. I'm always given it when visiting older relatives in the village.

SERVES 4

100ml olive oil
400g (2 large) onions, cut into chunks
2 tsp ground cinnamon
2 tsp ground cumin
1/2 tsp black pepper
500g (250g dried) cooked chickpeas (page xi)
250g coarse *burghul* (bulgur wheat)
1 tsp salt

Preparation time: 10 minutes, plus soaking overnight
Cooking time: 30 minutes, plus 1 hour to cook chickpeas

• Heat the oil and fry the onions until they start to turn a golden colour.

• Add the spices including the pepper and stir for 1 minute.

• Add the chickpeas and gently turn to coat with spices.

• Add the *burghul* and salt.

• Add just enough hot water to cover the surface of the *burghul* and bring to the boil, then cook over low heat for about 20 minutes to allow all the moisture to evaporate.

• Serve this dish with natural yogurt or salad, or both.

Cook's tip
• Sometimes this dish is cooked with long-grain rice instead of *burghul*. Prepare it in exactly the same way but remember to soak the rice for 1/2–1 hour (*burghul* never needs soaking).

Green Bean Stew

Yakhnet Loubeyeh

Loubeyeh is one of the most common vegetable dishes. It is served as a side dish or with rice as a main course. You can use any kind of green bean, depending on what's around and in season.

SERVES 4

1kg green beans
100ml olive oil
300g (2 medium) onions, chopped
60g (I bulb) garlic cloves
700g tomatoes, grated
1 tsp salt

Preparation time: 20 minutes
Cooking time: 40 minutes

• After trimming off the ends and removing any strings, cut the beans into pieces about 4cm long. Rinse in cold water and drain well.

• Heat half the oil and fry the onions to brown, then add the garlic and fry for another minute.

• Add the beans, then stir to mix with the onions and garlic. Cover the pan, turn the heat down to low and cook for 15 minutes to allow the beans to soften.

• Add the grated tomatoes and salt, cover and cook for another 15 minutes until the beans are very tender and the sauce has thickened.

• Remove from the heat and add the remaining oil.

• Serve with Lebanese Rice (page 264) or flat bread. Raw onions and peppers are also served as condiments with this dish.

Cook's tip
• If you are not serving the stew with rice as a main course, it is delicious served cold with bread.

Dried Bean Stew

Yakhnet Fasoulia

You can never go wrong with beans or get tired of eating them. In this recipe I used the small white beans, but it can be made with any other kind of beans you may prefer, which includes cannellini, haricot or butter beans.

SERVES 4

50ml olive oil
260g (1 large or 2 medium)
  onion, chopped
4 cloves garlic, crushed
1 tsp cinnamon
1 tsp salt
$\frac{1}{2}$ tsp black pepper
600g cooked (300g dried)
  beans (page xi)
50g tomato purée
30g chopped fresh coriander
About 500ml water

Preparation time: 15 minutes
Cooking time: 40 minutes,
  plus 1 hour if cooking
  dried beans

- Heat the oil and fry the onions to brown.

- Add garlic to the onions and fry for a minute, then add the cinnamon, salt and pepper and turn for another minute.

- Add the beans and tomato purée together with about 500ml water. Bring to the boil, turn the heat down, cover the pan and cook for about 30 minutes until the sauce has thickened.

- Add the coriander and simmer for a further 5 minutes.

- Serve with basmati or Lebanese Rice (page 264).

Cook's tip
- Beans tend to soak up a lot of moisture, so if you like more sauce in your food, just add a little more water before you remove the stew from the heat.

Okra Stew

Yakhnet Bameyeh

Okra is another popular vegetable in the Middle East, delicate and with an acquired taste. It is only cooked as a stew and never seems to be mixed with other vegetables.

SERVES 4

100ml olive oil
300g (2 medium) onions, coarsely chopped
8 cloves garlic, peeled
700g fresh okra, trimmed with tops cut off
450g tomatoes, diced
1 tbsp tomato purée
1 tsp ground cinnamon
$1/2$ tsp black pepper
1 tsp salt
50g fresh chopped coriander
1 tbsp pomegranate molasses or juice of 1 lemon

Preparation time: 20 minutes
Cooking time: 40 minutes

• Heat the oil and fry the onions and whole cloves garlic until they begin to brown.

• Add the okra, stir well, cover and simmer on low heat for 5 minutes, turning occasionally.

• Add the tomatoes, tomato purée, cinnamon, pepper and salt and simmer for another 15 minutes.

• Reserving a little to sprinkle on the top, add the fresh coriander to the pan. Simmer for a further 5 minutes until the sauce has thickened.

• Finally, add the pomegranate molasses or lemon juice and stir a little before turning out onto a serving dish.

• Sprinkle the remaining coriander over the top and serve with basmati or Lebanese Rice (page 264).

Vegetable Bake

Saneyeh Khoudra

This is a very common type of Lebanese dish, where all sorts of vegetables are mixed and cooked together. Absolutely no rules exist for this dish – you can use the vegetables of your choice or whatever you have in the house.

SERVES 4–6

70ml olive oil
400g (2 large) onions,
    chopped into chunks
2 tsp ground cinnamon
2 tsp salt
1 tsp ground black pepper
800g potatoes, peeled and
    cut into 3–4cm cubes
500g aubergines, cut into
    3–4cm cubes
700g courgettes, sliced
300g carrots, sliced
800g chopped tomatoes
50g tomato purée, diluted in
    100ml hot water

Preparation time: 15–20
    minutes
Cooking time: 45 minutes

• Heat the oil and fry the onions to soften and turn slightly golden. Stir in the cinnamon, salt and pepper.

• Add all the vegetables and tomatoes and turn to mix with the onions.

• Add the diluted tomato purée, cover the pot and cook for about 10 minutes.

• Preheat the oven to 220°C/425°F/gas mark 7.

• Turn the part-cooked vegetables into a shallow oven dish and bake in the preheated oven for 30–40 minutes until the surface is crispy (the crispiness adds a lot of flavour).

• Serve with Lebanese rice (page 264); some people prefer it just with bread.

Cook's tip
• Bake this dish in the shallowest baking tray you can find. You get more of the crispiness, which is what makes it so delicious.

Stuffed Baby Aubergines
Sheikh el Mehshi

Sheikh el Mehshi is another tasty aubergine dish, suitable for any day or occasion. It's easy to make and always looks impressive at a dinner party.

SERVES 4–6

1kg or about 15 baby aubergines

For the filling
50ml olive oil, plus extra if frying the aubergines
400g (2 large) onions, chopped
3 cloves garlic, chopped
250g carrots, diced
350g potatoes (very small), peeled and diced.
350g tomatoes, chopped
1 small red and 1 small green pepper, chopped
1 red chilli, deseeded and chopped (optional)
1/2 tsp ground black pepper
1 tsp ground cinnamon
1 tsp salt
Salt, to taste

For the sauce
80g tomato purée
400ml hot water
1 tsp salt

Preparation time: 15–20 minutes
Cooking time: 1 hour

• Trim the tops from the aubergines, leaving the stalks attached and peel half the skin away vertically so they look stripy.

• Either fry the aubergines in hot oil to brown them, or rub with oil and bake in an oven preheated to 230°C/450°F/gas mark 8. This may take about 20–30 minutes, depending on the oven.

• While the aubergines are roasting, make the filling. Heat the olive oil, fry the onions to brown and stir in the garlic for 1 minute.

• Preheat the oven to 220°C/425°F/gas mark 7, if not already using.

• Add the carrots, potatoes, tomatoes, peppers and chilli, if using, to the onion and garlic mixture. Cook for 15 minutes, then add the black pepper and cinnamon.

• Slit each aubergine lengthways and spoon in the vegetable filling, then place in a baking dish.

• Dilute the tomato purée with 400ml hot water and 1 teaspoon salt and pour over the stuffed aubergines.

• Bake in the preheated oven for about 30 minutes until the sauce has thickened.

• Serve with Lebanese Rice (page 264).

Upside Down Vegetable and Rice Cake
Makloubeh

Due to the presence of Palestinians in Lebanon, this dish has been added to the country's culinary repertoire. It is usually made either with aubergines or cauliflower, but I sometimes make it with both. Whichever way you choose, it will always be delicious and makes a lovely centrepiece.

SERVES 4–6

250g long-grain rice
Oil, for frying
700g (2 medium) aubergines, each cut into 6 wedges
700g cauliflower, cut into florets
550g (4 medium) onions, sliced
2 tsp cinnamon
1 tsp mixed spices (page 258)
½ tsp ground nutmeg
½ tsp ground black pepper
1 tsp salt
1 tomato, chopped

For garnish
25g roasted pine nuts (optional)
A little chopped parsley

Preparation time: 20 minutes
Cooking time: 1 hour, 10 minutes

• Rinse the rice and leave it to soak while preparing the following.

• Heat some oil (see tip opposite) and fry the aubergines and cauliflower to brown, then place on kitchen towels to absorb the oil. (You can bake these instead of frying, if you prefer. Place the cut vegetables on a greased oven tray, drizzle with oil and bake in an oven preheated to 230°C/450°F/gas mark 8 to brown for about 30 minutes for the aubergines and 45 minutes for the cauliflower.)

• With the same oil, fry the onions until they are slightly browned.

• Stir in the cinnamon, mixed spices, nutmeg, black pepper and salt and cook for 1 minute. Spread the chopped tomato over the onions (this is just to add a little colour).

• Spread the cauliflower and aubergines on top of the onions.

• Drain the rice and spread over the top of the vegetables. Add just enough water to be level with the rice and turn up the heat.

• When the water boils and starts to evaporate turn the heat down to low, cover the pan and cook for about 30 minutes until all the water has evaporated. Taste the rice and if it's still a bit crunchy, add a little more water and cook for another 5 minutes.

• Allow the *makloubeh* to rest for 5 minutes. Remove the lid and place your chosen serving dish or a large plate over it, then carefully turn the pot upside down, so the plate is on the bottom. Now slowly remove the pot.

• Garnish with pine nuts and parsley and serve *makloubeh* with natural yogurt as a sauce.

Cook's tip
• It is better to use a saucepan with small, round handles for this. A long handled saucepan will make it difficult to turn it upside down and have the *makloubeh* in a cake shape on the serving plate.

Pumpkin and Bulgur Wheat Pie

Kebbeh Lakteen Bil Saneyeh

Pumpkin is the vegetarian version for *kebbeh*, which is very popular among non-vegetarians, especially during the six weeks of Lent. It is very substantial and works well as a filling main dish, unlike *kebbeh* balls that are served as snacks or a side dish.

SERVES 6–8

For the kebbeh *dough*
1¹/₂kg pumpkin
350g fine *burghul* (bulgur wheat), rinsed and drained
1 medium onion, grated
40g white flour
Zest of 1 small orange
2 tsp ground cumin
1 tsp dried mint
1 tsp dried marjoram
1 tsp salt
¹/₂ tsp ground black pepper
1 tsp mixed spices (page 258)
3 tsp olive oil

For the filling
100ml olive oil
700g (3 large) onions, cut in half and sliced
400g cooked (200g dried) chickpeas (page xi)
1 heaped tsp cinnamon
1 tsp salt
¹/₂ tsp black pepper

Preparation time: 20 minutes
Cooking time: 1 hour 10 minutes

- To make the *kebbeh*, cut the pumpkin into halves, leaving the skin on, and remove the seeds. Cover with aluminium foil, place in a baking tray with little water in it, and bake in a hot oven (230°C/450°F/gas mark 8) for about half an hour.

- Remove from the oven and scoop out the flesh, which is easier than peeling the raw, hard skin. Mash the flesh and leave in a sieve to drain.

- To make the *kebbeh* dough, mix together all the remaining dough ingredients apart from the olive oil and allow to rest for half an hour.

- Preheat the oven to 220°C/425°F/gas mark 7.

- To make the filling, heat the olive oil and sauté the onions until they are slightly browned.

- Add the chickpeas, cinnamon, salt and black pepper, then stir well and cook on a low heat for 5 minutes.

- Grease a 30 x 25cm baking tray or the equivalent with little oil and spread half the *kebbeh* mixture evenly inside. Smooth with the palm of your hand.

- Spread the filling all over the layer of *kebbeh*.

- Take a handful of the remaining *kebbeh*, pat it flat, then place it on top of the filling. Repeat this method until you have covered all the filling and smooth with your hand until there are no cracks.

- Slice the top layer of the *kebbeh*, being careful not to cut through the bottom layer. Drizzle with 3 tablespoons of olive oil and bake for 30 minutes in the preheated oven.

- Serve with green salad.

Stuffed Chard Leaves

Mehshi Silq

Another stuffed vegetable dish, this one is however unique in both taste and style when served with a special tahini sauce mixed with chard stalks. For me it's the best.

SERVES 4–6

500g Swiss chard, stalks cut off and used for the sauce

For the filling
250g round rice, pudding rice, risotto rice, or sushi rice, soaked for 1 hour
150g cooked (75g dried) chickpeas (page xi)
80g chopped parsley
120g (1 medium) onion, chopped
15g chopped mint
300g tomatoes, chopped
50ml olive oil
Juice of 1 lemon
1 tsp salt

For the cooking sauce
500ml water, plus 20ml olive oil and ½ tsp salt

For the tahini sauce
The stalks from the chard leaves
Juice of 1 lemon
2 cloves garlic, crushed
200ml tahini
1 tsp salt

Preparation time: 40 minutes, plus soaking chickpeas overnight
Cooking time: 35–40 minutes, plus 1 hour to cook chickpeas

• Boil a little water and blanche the chard leaves by dipping them quickly in and out just to soften. Remove and place in a sieve to drain while preparing the filling.

• Rinse the rice, drain well and mix with all the remaining filling ingredients.

• On each chard leaf, place about 1 teaspoon of filling and roll firmly. Follow the steps for Stuffed Cabbage Leaves (page148).

• Place the rolls in a saucepan with the 500ml water mixed with olive oil and salt. Bring to the boil, turn the heat down to low, cover the pan and simmer for 30–40 minutes until the sauce has evaporated.

• Meanwhile, to make the tahini sauce, cook the chard stalks in boiling water for 5 minutes or until they become tender. Place in a sieve to drain; cut into 1–2cm pieces.

• Follow the method for tahini sauce (page 266) using the remaining ingredients.

• Add the chopped stalks to the sauce and mix well.

• Serve the stuffed leaves with the tahini and chard stalk sauce and lemon wedges.

Mixed Vegetable and Bean Stew

Fasoulia Ma Khoudra

This straightforward everyday dish can be served hot or cold and it's a great way to use up whatever vegetables you have around.

SERVES 4

100ml olive oil
250g ((2 medium)) onions, chopped
6 cloves garlic
250g courgette, cut into 3cm cubes
300g aubergine, cut into 3cm cubes
300g carrots, sliced
220g green beans, ends trimmed and cut into smaller pieces
250g cooked (125 dried) beans of any type (page xi)
250g mixed yellow and red peppers, deseeded and chopped
400g tomatoes, chopped
2 chillies, deseeded and chopped (optional)
2 tbsp tomato purée

Preparation time: 15 minutes
Cooking time: 45 minutes

• Heat half the oil and fry the onions and garlic to brown, reserving the remaining oil.

• Add all the remaining ingredients to the onions and stir-fry for few minutes, then cover the pan and turn the heat down.

• Cook the stew gently in its own juices for about 40 minutes, making sure you have a thick, rich sauce.

• Remove from the heat and stir in the remaining olive oil.

• Serve this dish with Lebanese Rice (page 264) or bread.

Cook's tip

• There are no rules to this dish – you can use any vegetables in season and add any other pulses you like. It can be served hot with rice or cold with pitta bread.

Cauliflower in Tahini and Coriander Sauce

Karnabeet Be Tahini

Tahini, made from sesame seeds, is such a rich ingredient, especially when cooked. The tahini sauce in this dish turns a cauliflower into a flavoursome, filling meal.

SERVES 4–6

1 large cauliflower (1–1¼ kg), divided into florets
30ml oil, plus a little to drizzle
500g (2 large) onions, sliced
6 cloves sliced garlic

For the sauce
Juice of 2 lemons
1 tsp salt
400ml tahini
40g coarsely chopped coriander

Ground chilli, for sprinkling (optional), or use paprika for colour

Preparation time: 20 minutes
Cooking time: 50 minutes

• Rinse the cauliflower, sprinkle with a little salt, drizzle with a little oil, and place on a shallow baking tray to allow browning. Bake in an oven preheated to 220°C/425°F/gas mark 7 for 30–40 minutes until it becomes slightly brown until tender.

• Heat 30ml oil and sauté the onions and garlic until soft and slightly brown.

• To make the tahini sauce, add the lemon juice and salt to the tahini and mix with a spoon until dry and fluffy. Adding a little cold water at a time, keep mixing until you have a thin, runny sauce (tahini will thicken when cooking). Taste for salt and add a little more, if liked.

• Saving a little coriander for the garnish, add the rest to the tahini sauce.

• Transfer the cauliflower to a deep ovenproof dish.

• Add the onions and garlic, pour the tahini sauce over the top and bake in the preheated oven for 20 minutes.

• Sprinkle with chilli or paprika and serve with Lebanese Rice (page 264) or plain rice and lemon wedges.

Baby Broad Beans with Rice

Foul Brouz

Everyone in Lebanon loves broad beans. There are many ways of cooking them, all very popular, as well as the option of eating them raw when fresh and in season. Around April and May, you will see many stalls on the roadside selling mountains of broad beans.

SERVES 4–6

250g basmati or long-grain rice
100ml olive oil
500g (2 large) onions, chopped
2 tsp ground cinnamon
2 tsp ground cumin
1 tsp salt
$^1/_2$ tsp ground black pepper
750g fresh or frozen baby broad beans
3 cloves garlic, crushed
40g chopped coriander

Preparation time: 10 minutes
Cooking time: 35 minutes

• Rinse the rice and leave it to soak for 30 minutes to 1 hour.

• Heat 70ml of the oil and fry the onions until golden brown.

• Add the cinnamon, cumin, salt and pepper and stir for a minute or two.

• Add the broad beans and mix in with the onions, then cover and simmer for 5 minutes.

• Add the rice and enough water to cover the top by 1cm. Bring to the boil and continue boiling until the water is level with the rice.

• Simmer on a low heat for about 20 minutes until all the moisture has evaporated.

• For the top dressing, heat the remaining 30ml of oil and stir in the garlic and coriander for 1 minute.

• Turn the rice out onto a flat serving dish and spread with the garlic and coriander over the top.

• Serve this dish with natural yogurt on the side.

Lentils with Rice

Mjadara

Mjadara is known as poor man's food but everyone loves it, and it's frequently cooked in Lebanese households. People always revert to *mjadara* when they can't decide what to cook on the day.

SERVES 4–6

500g green lentils
100ml olive oil
300g (2 medium) onions,
    chopped
60g long-grain rice or
    burghul (bulgur wheat)
2 tsp salt

Preparation time: 10 minutes
Cooking time: 1 hour, 20
    minutes

• Rinse the lentils and cook in 1 litre of water for about 40 minutes. Please refer to the packet instructions as the cooking time can vary. The lentils should be well cooked and you will need to add more water as necessary.

• Heat half the oil and fry the onions to brown, then add to the lentils.

• Add the rice and cook for another 20–30 minutes on a low heat until everything is well cooked and has taken on the consistency of a purée.

• When most of the moisture has evaporated, add the salt and turn off the heat, then stir in the remaining olive oil.

• Transfer to a serving dish and allow to set.

• Serve with Cabbage Salad (page 62) or any salad you prefer – Minty Yogurt and Cucumber Salad (page 74) also works well. *Mjadara* is always eaten with bread too.

Aubergines with Chickpeas
Mnazzaleh

Mnazzaleh is one of the very popular mountain dishes. Once unknown to many city people, in the last decade, like so many other traditional Lebanese dishes, it has become very popular.

SERVES 4–6

100ml olive oil
200–250g (1 large) onion, chopped
6 cloves whole garlic
2 medium aubergines, cut into cubes about 4cm square
400g tomatoes, chopped
60g tomato purée, diluted in 400ml water
1 tsp or more of salt
500g cooked (250g dried) chickpeas (page xi)

Preparation time: 10 minutes, plus soaking time
Cooking time: 50 minutes, plus 1 hour to cook chickpeas

• Heat half the oil and fry the onion and garlic to brown.

• Add the aubergines, tomatoes, diluted purée and salt.

• Cover the pan and cook on a medium heat for about 15 minutes.

• Add the chickpeas and cook for another 25 minutes until the sauce has thickened.

• After turning off the heat, add the remaining oil and stir gently.

• This dish is always served with bread. It can be served warm but is mostly served cold.

Ado/Taro Roots

Kilkass Be Tahini

This is another traditional peasant way of serving the delicious root vegetable *kilkass* (see also page 92).

SERVES 6–8

50ml olive oil
800g *kilkass* (taro or ado root), peeled and cut into small cubes
280g (2 medium) red onions, sliced
3 plump cloves of garlic, sliced
1 heaped tsp ground cumin
200ml Tahini Sauce (page 266)
1 tsp salt

Preparation time: 20 minutes
Cooking time: about 40 minutes

• Heat the oil and fry the taro or ado root cubes until golden brown. Remove from the heat and leave on kitchen towels.

• With the same oil, fry the onions and garlic until golden brown, then stir in the cumin.

• Make the tahini sauce as page 266.

• Return the *kilkass* to the pan with the onions, add the tahini sauce and salt. Stir until it begins to boil.

• Turn the heat to low and allow to simmer for 15 minutes. Tahini can become quite thick; if so, just add a little more water for a creamy sauce.

• This dish is usually eaten with bread. It can be served as a main dish with Cumin Rice (page 269).

Pea Stew

Yakhnet Bazella

Stews are a staple of Lebanese homely everyday food, all cooked in rich tomato sauce. As well as being enjoyed by adults, pea stew is loved by children, even the fussy eaters. When after school my children brought friends home for dinner, the young guests always requested pea stew.

SERVES 4

50ml olive oil
400g (2 large) onions, chopped
4–5 cloves garlic, crushed
1 tsp ground cinnamon
1 tsp salt
$^1/_2$ tsp ground black pepper
250g carrots, peeled and sliced
100g tomato purée
700ml hot water
700g fresh or frozen peas
Juice of 1 lemon
70g fresh coriander, chopped

Preparation time: 15 minutes
Cooking time: 40 minutes

• Heat the oil and fry the onions to brown. Add the garlic and fry for another minute, then add the cinnamon, salt and pepper. Stir with the onions for another minute.

• Add the carrots with the tomato purée and water. Allow to boil for a few minutes, then cover the pot and cook on medium heat for 10 minutes.

• Add the peas and lemon juice and cook for another 20 minutes.

• Reserving a little coriander, add the rest to the stew and cook for just 2 minutes.

• Sprinkle the remaining coriander over the top of the stew just before serving.

• Serve with Lebanese Rice (page 264) or basmati rice.

Cook's tip
• Lemon juice is often added to the dish but you can serve lemon wedges on the side, if you prefer.

Rolled Vine Leaves

Mehshi Warak Inab

Stuffed vine leaves are often cooked at home and served with other stuffed vegetables. They are great to serve at dinner parties as part of a buffet and always served in restaurants as one of the *maza* (starters) selection. You may find them quite fiddly at first, but it only gets easier and quicker the more you make them.

SERVES 4

2 tomatoes, sliced
300g fresh vine leaves or
  500g in brine
250g pudding or Italian
  risotto rice, soaked for
  30 minutes or more
140g chopped flat-leaf
  parsley
30g chopped fresh mint
400g tomatoes, chopped
100g spring onions, trimmed
  and chopped
Juice of 2 lemons
1 tsp salt
50ml olive oil, plus 30ml for
  the sauce

Preparation time: 1 hour
Cooking time: 40 minutes

• Line the bottom of a pan with the sliced tomatoes.

• Blanch the vine leaves in boiling water and drain, if using fresh. If using leaves in brine, rinse well in fresh water to reduce the salt content.

• To make the filling, drain the rice and mix well with the remaining ingredients, except for the 30ml of oil needed for the cooking sauce. Allow to rest for 20 minutes for the rice to absorb the juices.

• Place the shiny side of the vine leaves face down and put 1–2 teaspoons of filling on the matte side of each leaf. Fold the sides over the filling, then fold over the top end nearest to you and roll firmly towards the end of the leaf. Place them in the pan on top of the sliced tomatoes.

• Add water to finish just level with the rolled leaves.

• Bring to a boil for few minutes, then add the remaining oil. Cover the pan, turn the heat down and simmer for about 30 minutes until the water has evaporated. Test a vine leaf to make sure the rice is well cooked.

• If serving vine leaves as a main dish, serve with plain yogurt on the side and some bread.

Cook's tip
• You can prepare the rolled vine leaves or cook them in advance, as they are always served cold or slightly warm.

Rice and Lentils with Caramelized Onions
Mdardara

One of the most popular lentil dishes, *Mdardara* is always served as a main meal. The caramelized onions spread over the top add a wonderful flavour.

SERVES 4–6

250g green lentils
100ml olive oil
3 large onions, halved and
   sliced
150g long-grain rice, soaked
   for $^1/_2$ –1 hour
1 tsp salt

Preparation time: 10 minutes
Cooking time: 1 hour

• Pour hot water over the lentils and leave for about 30 minutes, until they are just cooked but not too soft. Drain, reserving the stock.

• While the lentils are cooking, heat the oil and fry the onions until brown. Remove half the onions and continue to cook the remainder until they are crispy brown; spread out on kitchen paper to remove the excess oil.

• Drain the soaked rice, add the non-crispy onions and salt. Cover the rice with the reserved stock from the lentils. Cook for 10 minutes until most of the water has evaporated.

• Fold the lentils in with the rice and cook for a further 10 minutes.

• After turning the *mdardara* out onto a serving plate, spread the crispy onions to cover the top.

• Serve this dish with plain yogurt or Minty Yogurt and Cucumber Salad (page 74) and Tomato Salad (page 76).

Cook's tip
• This is a lovely dish to have in your fridge for quick meals or snacks. My children make a large batch of *mdardara,* so there is always food ready to eat.

Aubergine Bake

Saneyet Batingane

With its lovely combination of flavours, this dish always goes down well with the whole family. Even if you prepare it the day before it will only improve.

SERVES 4–6

3 aubergines, cut into 2cm
  thick slices
50ml olive oil
Salt
120g green lentils
300g (2 medium) onions,
  chopped
700g sweet potatoes, peeled
  and cut into cubes
400g feta cheese
300g fresh tomatoes,
  chopped
3 cloves garlic, crushed
30g chopped parsley
Ground black pepper
50g tomato purée

Preparation time: 30 minutes
Cooking time: 30 minutes,
  plus 25 minutes' baking

• Grease an oven tray, place the aubergine slices on it, drizzle with oil and sprinkle with a little salt. Bake in an oven preheated to 230°C/450°F/gas mark 8 to brown for about 20 minutes. However, most people prefer to fry the aubergines in a little oil.

• At the same time, cook the lentils. Add boiling water, cover and cook for about 30–40 minutes, making sure they are well cooked. Drain the lentils and reserve the stock.

• While preparing the lentils and the aubergines, make the filling. Heat the olive oil and fry the onions to brown slightly.

• Add the sweet potatoes, turn with the onions, then lower the heat, cover the pan and simmer for 15–20 minutes until the potatoes are cooked.

• Turn down the oven to 220°C/425°F/gas mark 7.

• Crumble the cheese with your fingers and add to the sweet potatoes, together with the lentils, tomatoes, garlic, parsley, 1 teaspoons salt and some pepper. Mix well.

• Line an oven dish with half the aubergines, spread the filling evenly on top and cover with the remaining aubergines.

• Dilute the tomato purée with the lentil stock, pour over the top and bake for 25 minutes in the preheated oven.

• Serve with a crispy green salad.

Cook's tip
• Not everyone likes sweet potatoes but you can replace with regular potatoes, if you prefer.

Walnut Tortellini in Yogurt Sauce

Shish Barak

Shish barak is one of the traditional dishes that never went out of fashion. Natural yogurt is frequently used in Lebanese kitchens either for cooking, dressings or salads, or concentrated for dips and spreading. In this recipe the tortellini are cooked in the yogurt sauce; indeed, tortellini is never cooked in any other sauce in Lebanon. It is more time-consuming to make than most dishes, but I really believe it's worth it.

SERVES 4

150g flour, plus a little for
 rolling out
Salt
100g long-grain rice
50ml oil
60g butter
400g (2 large) onions,
 chopped
1 tsp ground cinnamon
Ground black pepper
100g finely chopped walnuts
1 tbsp cornflour, combined
 with 200ml cold water
2ltr natural yogurt
4 cloves garlic, crushed
50g chopped coriander
A little paprika (optional)

Preparation time: 1 hour
Cooking time: 1 hour

• Make the dough by mixing the flour with a little salt. Continue mixing, while adding a little cold water at a time, to form a dough. Cover and then leave in the fridge for 30 minutes.

• Cook the rice according to the packet instructions and drain.

• To make the filling, heat the oil and 30g of the butter and fry the onions to brown. Add the cinnamon, a little salt and pepper and stir for 1 minute. Then mix in the walnuts and set aside to cool.

• Add the cornflour paste to the yogurt and heat, stirring continuously, until it begins to boil. Turn the heat down to low and add the rice and 1 teaspoon of salt. Continue to cook for about 20 minutes, giving it the occasional stir.

• Meanwhile, make the tortellini by rolling out the dough and cutting circles about 6cm in diameter with a pastry cutter (see step pictures).

• Put 1 teaspoon of the filling into the centre of each circle, fold over and squeeze the edges to stick together. Now you have a half circle shape. twist one corner to overlap with the other corner and squeeze to seal the tortellini.

• Now the yogurt has reduced and the rice has almost disintegrated, drop the tortellini into the yogurt one by one, making sure they are separated, and cook for another 20 minutes.

- Heat the remaining butter, add the garlic and stir until it begins to change colour. Add the coriander (reserving a little for the garnish) and gently stir for a few seconds. Add to the yogurt and tortellini and cook for another 2 minutes.

- Garnish with the remaining coriander and a sprinkle of paprika (optional).

- This dish is usually served on its own.

Potato Stew

Yakhnet Batata

As I mentioned earlier, the Lebanese love stews. They are always served with rice, even this potato version. You may think it's an all-carbs dinner, but that's the way it is! Let yourself go with this meal and make up for the vegetable intake with the next one. It's delicious.

SERVES 4

50ml olive oil
250g (2 medium) onions, chopped
4–5 cloves garlic, crushed
1 tsp ground cinnamon
$^1/_2$ tsp black pepper
1 tsp salt
1kg potatoes, peeled and cut into cubes
80g tomato purée
30g chopped coriander

Preparation time: 15 minutes
Cooking time: 40 minutes

• Heat the oil and fry the onions to brown.

• Add the garlic, cinnamon, pepper and salt. Stir for 1 minute.

• Add the potato cubes and enough water to cover, together with the tomato purée. Bring to the boil, cover the pan, turn the heat down to medium and cook for 25–30 minutes until the potatoes are cooked and the sauce has thickened.

• Keeping a little for garnishing, add the remaining coriander and cook for another 2 minutes.

• Serve with Lebanese Rice (page 264).

Cook's tip
• This is one of the few dishes that is better cooked and served straight away, as potatoes tend to change in texture when left in sauce for longer. If you serve this to young children, they tend to love it, too.

Poached Eggs in Tahini

Shamahleyeh

This tasty recipe, from my childhood, has been forgotten by my generation and most young people have never even heard of it. When staying with my Aunt Souraya in the mountains, she always made this for us, especially when we turned up unexpectedly as she is one of those people who has to feed whoever steps into her house. It is made with ingredients you always have in the cupboard.

SERVES 4

Juice of 1 large lemon (50ml)
300g tahini
700ml water
50ml cooking oil
250g (2 medium) onions, cut
  in half and thinly sliced
1 tsp salt
4 cloves garlic, crushed
8 eggs

Preparation time: 10 minutes
Cooking time: 45 minutes

• In a bowl, mix the lemon juice with the tahini until it becomes fluffy. Adding a little water at a time, keep mixing until all the water is blended with the tahini and there are no lumps. The tahini sauce in this recipe needs to be thin.

• Heat the oil and sauté the onions until slightly brown.

• Pour the tahini sauce over the onions, add the salt and garlic and while stirring all the time, heat until it comes to the boil. Turn down the heat and giving it the occasional stir, cook for 10 minutes until the mixture becomes creamy.

• Remove from the heat to stop the tahini bubbling, then break each egg into the tahini, keeping them separated. Leave to stand for a few minutes, hopefully keeping the white firmly round the yolk.

• Return to the heat and cook for another 20 minutes until the yolks are firm.

• Add a little more water if the tahini becomes too thick; it should have a creamy texture.

• Serve with Lebanese Rice (page 264).

Cook's tip
• I hope you will try this unique recipe. It is seriously good. If prepared in advance, tahini can thicken, so add a little water when reheating to thin the sauce.

Stuffed Vegetables

Mahashi

Everyone loves stuffed vegetables, including small children. It is such a family dish, as well as being always presented at dinner parties. It's hard to give you the exact preparation time the first time you make this but it becomes quicker each time you make it. You will need a special tool for scooping out the inside of the vegetables (a *mankara*), which can be bought online or in Middle Eastern shops.

SERVES 4

1kg baby aubergines
1kg small courgettes (or
　longer ones cut in half)
250g small green peppers,
　ends cut off and deseeded
Salt
1 tbsp olive oil

For the filling
325g fresh tomatoes,
　chopped
120g spring onions, trimmed
　and chopped
100g chopped parsley
25g chopped mint
50ml lemon juice
50ml olive oil
1 tsp salt
250g pudding or risotto rice,
　soaked for 1 hour

Preparation time: 45
　minutes, plus 1 hour
　soaking rice
Cooking time: 45 minutes

• To make the filling, add the tomatoes, onions, parsley, mint, lemon juice, olive oil and 1 teaspoon of salt to the rice. Mix well and allow to rest for 15 minutes.

• Before cutting off the tops of the aubergines, roll them firmly with your hand on a flat surface to soften in the middle. This will make scooping out the flesh much easier.

• After cutting off the tops of the courgettes, aubergines and peppers, gently work the scoop (*mankara*) in and turn it like a screw, making sure you don't go through the bottom of the vegetable. Even if you do, you can still use the broken vegetable. The shell should be about 1cm thick or less.

• Fill two-thirds of the vegetables with the filling, so there is enough room for the rice to expand.

• Place everything in a saucepan, add about 800ml of water with a little salt and 1 tbsp olive oil.

• Bring to the boil, then reduce the heat, cover the pan and cook for about 45 minutes.

• I always take one vegetable out to test, just to make sure the rice is well cooked before serving.

• Serve with plain yogurt on the side.

Cook's tip
• Most people don't have the ingredients to make the exact amount of filling for the prepared vegetables and end up with some left over. If I have extra filling, I stuff tomatoes, onions, potatoes or whatever I have in the house. It's up to you!

Arabian Nutty Rice

Kabseh

The Lebanese have adapted this Saudi Arabian national dish. There are so many versions but cardamom is the main flavour. The long list of ingredients may look scary, but they are very basic and there is no waste. Add other favourite nuts if you like.

SERVES 4–6

60ml oil, plus extra to fry the nuts
200g (1 large) onion, finely chopped
1 heaped tsp mixed spices (page 258)
1 tsp ground cardamom
I heaped tsp ground cumin
1 tsp salt
$^1/_2$ tsp ground black pepper
350g carrots, diced
1 large red pepper, deseeded and chopped
1 large green pepper, deseeded and chopped
2 cloves garlic, crushed
350g basmati rice, soaked for 30 minutes–1 hour
100g split or flaked almonds
50g cashew nuts
30g pine nuts

For the sauce
50ml oil
200g (1 large) onion, chopped
650g chopped tomatoes
2 hot red chillies, deseeded and sliced
2 plump cloves garlic, crushed
1 tsp salt

Preparation time: 20 minutes
Cooking time: 40 minutes

• Heat the oil and fry the onion to brown slightly. Add the spices, salt and pepper and fry with the onions for 1 minute.

• Add the carrots, red and green peppers. Stir-fry for 5 minutes, then add the crushed garlic.

• Drain and add the rice to the vegetables, add salt and enough water to cover the rice by no more than 1cm. Allow it to boil until most of the water has evaporated on the surface.

• Turn the heat to low and simmer for about 20 minutes until all the moisture has evaporated.

• Heat some oil and fry the cashews and almonds to brown, then remove from the oil and set aside. Fry the pine nuts in the same oil to brown, keeping an eye on them because they turn brown very quickly. Set the nuts aside on kitchen paper.

• Turn the rice out onto a serving dish and sprinkle the nuts over the top.

• To make the sauce, heat the oil and fry the onion until it turns golden brown.

• Add the tomatoes, chillies, garlic and salt. Cover the pan and simmer on low heat for about 15–20 minutes.

• Serve the rice with the tomato sauce. Some people prefer it with natural yogurt as well as or instead of the sauce.

Spinach with Rice

Sbanekh Ma Rouz

In Lebanon everyone (almost) likes spinach because it is never served plain as a side vegetable. It is cooked as a main dish and always served with rice, used as rolled leaves and to make spinach triangles (page 128) Pine nuts work really well in this dish but if you don't have any, it's still good without them.

SERVES 4

50g butter
350g onions (about 2 large),
   chopped
4 cloves garlic
60g chopped coriander
1kg chopped spinach,
   washed and drained (you
   may use frozen spinach)
1 tsp salt
$1/2$ tsp black pepper
30g pine nuts
Juice of 1 lemon

For the yogurt sauce
500g natural yogurt
2 cloves garlic, crushed
30g chopped fresh mint
Salt, to taste

Preparation time: 20 minutes
Cooking time: 30–35
   minutes

• Melt 30g of the butter and fry the onions until golden brown.

• Slice 2 cloves garlic and fry with the onions for 2 minutes.

• Add half the coriander to the spinach and stir-fry with the onions, garlic and the salt. Leave to simmer until all the water from the spinach has evaporated.

• Melt the remaining butter, crush the other 2 garlic cloves into it and stir together with the rest of the coriander for 1–2 minutes. Add to the spinach mixture, stir and cook for another minute. Add the lemon juice.

• For the yogurt sauce, just mix all the ingredients together. Serve with the spinach mixture on a bed of Lebanese Rice (page 264).

• Sprinkle nuts over the top when serving, if liked.

Bulgur Wheat with Vegetables

Burghul Bkhudra

My mother and her sisters were very resourceful with food. They managed to knock up a tasty meal with whatever there was in the house. *Burghul* is always available in every Lebanese household and is quick to cook. By adding vegetables, you can turn it into a meal in half an hour.

SERVES 4

50ml olive oil
270g (2 medium) onions, diced
3 cloves garlic, chopped
200g carrots, chopped
250g courgettes, cut into small cubes
200g mixed coloured peppers, deseeded chopped or diced
350g tomatoes, chopped
1 tsp salt
1 tsp mixed spices (page 258)
130g coarse *burghul* (bulgur wheat), preferably wholemeal, if available
A little chopped parsley, to garnish

Preparation time: 15 minutes
Cooking time: 20 minutes

• Heat the oil and fry the onions to brown; stir in the garlic for 1 minute.

• Add all the vegetables and stir-fry with the onions for 5 minutes then add the tomatoes, salt and mixed spices. Stir on the heat for 1 minute.

• Rinse, drain and add the *burghul* and just enough water to cover the surface. Allow it to boil for a minute, then turn down the heat to low, cover the pan and simmer until all the water has evaporated.

• Sprinkle with chopped parsley and serve with Minty Yogurt and Cucumber Salad (page 74) or simply plain yogurt.

Cook's tip
• You can use the vegetables of your choice in this recipe. As with any *burghul* recipe, it is always better cooked when ready to serve.

Filled Artichoke Hearts

Mehshi Ardi Showki

Artichokes are very popular in Lebanon when in season. They are used in salads, served with lemon and oil dressing or stuffed and baked either in a lemon, as here, or tomato sauce.

SERVES 4–6

12 frozen artichoke hearts (no defrosting required)
Salt
50ml oil
350g (2 medium) onions, cut in half and thinly sliced
60g crushed walnuts
A little ground black pepper
30g butter
25g plain flour
350ml water
30ml lemon juice, plus juice of ^{1}/$_2$ lemon for boiling the artichokes
A little chopped parsley, to garnish

Preparation time: 10 minutes
Cooking time: 35 minutes, plus 40 minutes' baking

• Add 2 tsp salt and the juice of ^{1}/$_2$ lemon to a pan of boiling water, cook the artichokes for 10–15 minutes, then drain. The lemon juice in the boiling water prevents them from turning brown.

• Preheat the oven to 200°C/400°F/gas mark 6.

• To make the filling, heat the oil and sauté the onions until they turn slightly brown. Add the walnuts, ^{1}/$_2$ teaspoon salt and the pepper, stir and remove from the heat.

• For the sauces, melt the butter, add the flour and stir for 2 minutes, then gradually add a little water at a time. Keep stirring until it has all been added. Stir in the lemon juice and ^{1}/$_2$ teaspoon salt.

• Fill each one of the artichoke hearts with the onion and walnut mixture, and place in an oven dish.

• Pour the lemon sauce over the filled artichokes.

• Bake in the preheated oven for 40 minutes until the tops of the artichokes are slightly crispy.

• Garnish with a sprinkle of chopped parsley for a touch of colour.

• Serve with basmati or Lebanese Rice (page 264).

Cook's tip
• Most people prefer to shallow fry the artichoke hearts in a little oil for a few minutes to brown slightly before filling them, particularly when they are fresh, to add to the flavour.

Southern Red Lentil Mjadara

Mjadara Hamra Jnoubeyeh

This dish is a speciality of southern Lebanon. There are other versions of *mjadra* but the Southern way is certainly different and delicious in its own way. Red lentils are smaller than green ones. They are more brown than red but are referred to as red.

SERVES 4

150g red lentils
100ml olive oil
450g (2 large) onions, cut in
  half and sliced
160g coarse *burghul* (bulgur
  wheat), wholewheat if
  available
1 tsp salt
$^1/_2$ tsp black pepper

Preparation time: 10 minutes
Cooking time: 1 hour

• Cook the lentils in 1 litre of water for about 35 minutes, depending on the variety, being careful not to overcook them. Remove and save some of the stock for later.

• Meanwhile, heat the oil and sauté the onions until they become light brown. Add two-thirds of the onions to the lentils and cook for 10 minutes. Continue to fry the remaining onions until they are crispy and brown.

• Rinse the *burghul* and add to the lentils. Add the salt, pepper and some of the reserved stock, if needed, to bring it level with the lentils and *burghul*.

• When the mixture begins to boil, cover and lower the heat. Simmer for about 20 minutes, stirring once or twice, until all the moisture has evaporated.

• Turn the red *mjadra* out onto a serving dish and spread crispy onions over the top.

• Serve this dish with a bowl of natural yogurt or tomato salad (usually it is preferred cold).

Cook's tip
• There is a similar version of this recipe, but cooked with rice, commonly used throughout Lebanon. This southern version tastes completely different and is always the way it is served in the South.

Bean Mjadara

Mjadara Fasoulia

Mjadara is usually cooked with lentils and rice. This is a different version, made with beans instead of lentils. For this dish you can use any variety of bean.

SERVES 4

400g (200g dried) cooked beans, drained (page xi)
100ml olive oil
200g (1 large) onion, chopped
3 cloves garlic, crushed
1 tsp salt

Preparation time: 5–10 minutes
Cooking time: 40 minutes, if the beans are already cooked

- Soak the beans overnight, drain and boil for about an hour until they are very soft in the middle. (You may use tinned beans to save time.)

- Heat half the oil, add the onion and fry to brown.

- Add the garlic and stir with the onion for 1 minute.

- Drain the beans, add to the onions and top with just enough hot water to cover the surface of the beans.

- Cover and simmer on low heat for about 30 minutes, until most of the moisture has evaporated.

- Add the salt and roughly mash the beans with a fork in the pan, then cook for another 5 minutes. Most people use a blender but I prefer to have a coarse texture.

- Remove from the heat and add the remaining oil.

- Serve with any salad and bread.

Aubergines with Bulgur Wheat and Chickpeas

Kebbeh Batingane

As I've mentioned, the Lebanese love food; always they are either eating or talking about it. One day at the hairdresser's, I couldn't stop listening to the other women talking about aubergine *kebbeh*. It appealed to me as I'd never heard of it before. I joined in the conversation and as soon as I got home, I made it. I liked it so much that I've made it many times since.

SERVES 4–6

For the kebbeh dough
150g fine *burghul* (bulgur wheat)
250g cooked (125g dried) and crushed chickpeas (page xi)
125g (1 medium) onion, grated
1 tsp dried mint
1 tsp marjoram
1 tsp dried basil
1 tsp ground cumin
½ tsp mixed spices (page 258)
1 tsp salt
½ tsp black pepper

For the filling
100ml oil, for frying
400g (2 large) onions, chopped
600g (1 large) aubergine, peeled and cut into small pieces
30g pine nuts or chopped walnuts
2tsp ground sumac
1 tsp salt
50ml olive oil, for drizzling

Preparation time: 30 minutes
Cooking time: 25 minutes, plus 30 minutes' baking (plus 1 hour to cook chickpeas)

• Rinse the *burghul*, drain and then mix with all the *kebbeh* dough ingredients. You will need to add a little water if the dough mixture is too stiff.

• Allow the *kebbeh* to rest while preparing the filling.

• Preheat the oven to 220°C/425°F/gas mark 7.

• Heat the oil and fry the onions until they begin to turn brown. Add the aubergine pieces and sauté with the onions until soft, then add the pine nuts, sumac and salt.

• Grease a baking tray measuring roughly 25 x 25cm; slightly bigger will be fine, too.

• Evenly spread half the *kebbeh* dough across the base of the tin, then spread the filling on top.

• Taking a handful of *kebbeh*, flatten it between the palm of your hands and place it over the filling, repeat until you cover all the filling, smoothing the surface with wet hands so all unfilled gaps in the *kebbeh* are filled.

• Drizzle with olive oil and bake in the preheated oven for 30 minutes.

• Serve warm with plain yogurt or salad.

CHAPTER 7

Sweets

Hilwayat

Desserts in Lebanon are rarely served after a meal. Fresh fruit is preferred, and is very popular, and maybe a bite of something sweet such as a mouthful of fig or quince jam or some dates. Sweets are very popular but eaten at other times and often offered to guests with coffee.

There are many patisseries in the towns and cities, on almost every street, and, surprisingly, they all do well. It is the norm in Lebanon to call at a patisserie on the way to visit friends and family and to take along a selection of *baklawa* (baklava) or cakes and pastries. Not many people make desserts at home as they can buy them at such high quality.

Baklawa is traditionally offered at special occasions such as weddings and other celebrations. A wide selection is available. Even though they are made with the same ingredients, they come in different shapes and sizes and, oddly enough, they all taste different.

Although baklava is the most well known around the world, there are many more desserts on offer in Lebanon. I have selected a variety of traditional recipes; some are very old and others are desserts that are not available from patisseries.

Mazaher (orange blossom water) and *maward* (rose water) are low-cost and essential ingredients for making Lebanese desserts. They can be bought in Middle Eastern stores or online. But remember, do not be overgenerous with *mazaher* and *maward*: they are strongly flavoured and will ruin your dish if you are heavy-handed.

Syrupy Filo and Nut Pastries

Baklawa

Baklawa is the most common of the Middle Eastern sweet pastries. It is always offered to guests on special occasions and at celebrations. Because the baklawa sold in the many patisseries is so good, it is rare for people to bake it at home and often they don't realize how simple it is to make. Desserts in Lebanon are usually served with a selection of fresh fruits.

SERVES 6

300g walnuts, chopped in a processor to resemble breadcrumbs
40g sugar
1 tbsp *mazaher* (orange blossom water)
1 tbsp *maward* (rose water)
400g melted unsalted butter
270g packet of filo pastry, fresh or frozen
200ml cold Aromatic Sugar Syrup (page 266)
20g ground pistachios

Preparation time: 25 minutes
Cooking time: 45 minutes

Cook's tip
• You can use other varieties of nuts for the filling; it is very popular made with pistachios. I recommend keeping *baklawa* in a covered container in the fridge because the home-made ones don't tend to stay fresh as long as ready-made *baklawa*.

• Mix the walnuts with sugar, *mazaher and maward.*

• Grease a 25 x 20 x 5cm baking tray with melted butter.

• Unfold the filo sheets and cut across the middle to halve. Spread the first sheet across the base of the tin and brush with butter. Lay another sheet on top of the first one and again brush with butter, then continue until you have used a third of the sheets.

• Spread the walnut mix smoothly over the top and continue layering the remaining filo sheets in the same way as above.

• Brush the remaining butter over the surface of the baklava. Place in the fridge for 10 minutes so the butter sets, which makes cutting simpler.

• Preheat the oven to 180°C/350°F/gas mark 4.

• Slice the baklava into diamond shapes, using a sharp knife and cutting right through to the bottom of the layers of filo. Bake in the preheated oven for 45 minutes until the surface is golden brown.

• Remove from the oven, pour the cold syrup over the top and leave in the tin to soak it up.

• Remove the baklava pieces from the tin and sprinkle each one with ground pistachios.

Date and Tahini Balls

Tamer Be Tahini

Dates are frequently eaten in the Middle East, served with coffee, in pastry fillings or simply enjoyed on their own. One time, I was watching friends dipping dates in the tahini jar and thinking, why spoil the flavour of the dates? I reluctantly tried it and was surprised by what a lovely combination it made. I worked on this recipe, finally achieving the right balance.

MAKES 25–30

120g almonds
375g dates, pitted
70g tahini
4 tbsp water

Suggested coatings
20g sesame seeds
20g desiccated, unsweetened
  coconut
25g chopped pistachio nuts
25g chopped almonds

Preparation time: 45 minutes

• Blitz the almonds in a food processor until they resemble breadcrumbs.

• Mix the dates, tahini and 4 tbsp of water together, blending until they form a paste and then combine with the almonds.

• Dry-roast the sesame seeds in a frying pan and keep stirring until they turn slightly brown, if using for coating. Pour them onto a plate to cool.

• Roll the date mixture between the palms of your hands into balls about 3–4cm in diameter, then roll in one of the coating ingredients.

• Place the truffle-like date balls in the fridge to set for about 1 hour before serving.

Cook's tips
• A lovely treat to serve at Christmas time, these will keep for few weeks in an airtight container so they don't dry out. Serve with tea and coffee.

• It helps if your coatings are poured onto plates so you can easily roll the balls around and ensure they are fully covered.

Simple Milk Dessert

Mhallabeyeh

This uncomplicated dessert is bursting with flavours. It is very popular in Lebanon, affordable enough for any family to have as frequently as they wish, and it is often served in cafés as well as good restaurants.

SERVES 4

50g cornflour
80g sugar
800ml whole milk
1 tbsp orange blossom water
 (*mazaher*)
1/2 tsp ground mastic
 (*miskeh*), about 10–12
 crystals, if available (see
 also pages 10–12)
80g chopped almonds
 (optional)
30g crushed pistachios

Preparation time: 5 minutes
Cooking time: 15 minutes

- In a saucepan, dissolve the cornflour and sugar in the milk and bring to a boil, stirring continuously to avoid lumps forming.

- When the mixture thickens, add the *mazaher* and mastic and stir well.

- Remove at once from the heat, add almonds, if using, and pour into serving dishes.

- Allow to cool and then sprinkle crushed pistachios on top of each one.

- Refrigerate for up to 2 days.

Cook's tip
- If using mastic, place the crystals between two layers of greaseproof paper or a small plastic bag and crush with a rolling pin. They are easily crushed within a few seconds.

Cheese and Semolina Wraps

Halawet el Jiben

This delicious dessert is a speciality of north Lebanon. It is traditional to go to Tripoli (the capital city of the North) to indulge in this dessert, which is topped with aromatic syrup. As Lebanese, we will travel the country to eat where certain foods are best.

SERVES 4

1 x 220g ball of mozzarella cheese
25g semolina
2 tbsp rose water (*maward*)
1 tbsp aromatic Sugar Syrup (page 266), plus extra for rolling the cheese and serving
100g *kashta* (milk curd, page 267), mixed with 30g whipped cream
1 tbsp ground pistachio nuts
Candied orange petals (optional, see also page 10)

Preparation time: 30 minutes
Cooking time: 5–10 minutes

• Crumble the cheese into a saucepan and allow it to melt over low heat.

• Add the semolina, rose water and 1 tbsp of the syrup. Mix well over the heat for a few minutes until all the moisture has been absorbed into the semolina. It should resemble a ball of dough.

• Rub the syrup lightly over a worktop, and place the semolina dough on top. Quickly roll out the dough while it's still warm so that it spreads easily into a very thin sheet.

• Cut into 5 x 10cm pieces, put 1 heaped teaspoon of *kashta* in the centre of each one and roll into a little wrap.

• Place on a serving plate, sprinkle ground pistachios over the top and garnish with candied orange petals, if using.

• Serve with aromatic syrup on the side.

Cook's tip
• Sometimes this recipe is served shredded into small uneven strips and served with curd and syrup on the side.

Lebanese Curcum Yellow Cake

Sfoof

This is another traditional recipe that has never been forgotten. This aromatic pastry is still sold in shops but many people prefer to make it at home. The bright yellow colour comes from the turmeric (*curcum*).

SERVES 6

A few sesame seeds or pine
  nuts, to decorate
175g semolina
150g plain flour
280g sugar
1 tsp baking powder
2–3 tsp turmeric
250ml cooking oil
50ml olive oil
200ml milk
50ml *mazaher* (orange
  blossom water)
1 tbsp tahini, for greasing

Preparation time: 15–20
  minutes
Cooking time: 50 minutes

• Preheat the oven to 180°C/350°F/gas mark 4.

• Prepare the sesame seeds or pine nuts, if using, by dry-roasting them in a frying pan to brown. Keep turning until they brown.

• Mix together all the dry ingredients, then add the cooking oil, olive oil, milk and *mazaher*.

• Whisk everything together with an electric whisk for 1 minute.

• Grease a baking tray measuring approximately 22 x 32cm with the tahini and pour in the cake mixture.

• Sprinkle with sesame seeds or pine nuts and bake in the preheated oven for 50 minutes

• Allow the cake to cool, before cutting it into squares and removing from the tin.

Cook's tip
• Keep an eye on the pan when roasting the sesame or pine nuts seeds as they burn very easily, and will continue to cook even after you have turned off the heat.

Lebanese Fruit Salad

Cocktail Fwakeh

Fruit salad is usually a refreshing, quick and easy dessert. However, the Lebanese don't really believe in 'simple', even when making fruit salad – it has to be dressed up, but take my word, it's delicious! I like to use whatever fresh fruits are in season. The recipe here is just a guideline but of course you can use whatever is available or the fruits you prefer.

SERVES 4

130g nectarines
1 peach
150g grapes
7 green or red figs
250g melon
100g pomegranate seeds
15g pine nuts
1 tbsp *mazaher* (orange blossom water)
200g *kashta* (milk curd, page 267), mixed with 20g whipped cream
3 tbsp honey

Preparation time: 15–20 minutes

• Peel and cut into small pieces all the fruit you have chosen, removing any stones as necessary.

• Add the pine nuts (reserving a few for the topping) and *mazaher*, then leave in the fridge to absorb the flavours for 1–2 hours if you have the time. The fruit will naturally produce its own juice.

• Divide the fruit salad into 4 serving glasses, top with the *kashta* and drizzle with honey.

• Decorate with the remaining pine nuts and serve.

Cook's tip
• You can use crushed pistachios instead of pine nuts for the topping, if you prefer.

Syrupy Almond Fingers

Asabe Lowz

Almond fingers come from the *baklawa* family, but they are quicker and even easier to make. This recipe will definitely be enough for more than 4 people; it's difficult to judge with sweets. Of course, you can always halve the recipe.

SERVES 4–6

150g chopped almonds
50g sugar
2 tsp almond essence
270g packet filo pastry
60g melted butter or
  margarine
100ml aromatic Sugar Syrup
  (page 266)
15g ground pistachios

Preparation time: 20 minutes
Baking time: 25 minutes

• Roast the almonds in a dry pan, turning all the time because nuts tend to catch and burn, then put them in a food processor and blitz to resemble coarse breadcrumbs.

• Preheat the oven to 160°C/325°F/gas mark 3.

• Mix the nuts with the sugar and almond essence.

• Take a sheet of pastry and brush with melted butter. Sprinkle with 1 dessertspoon of the nut filling and firmly roll up all the way to the end of the sheet. Repeat with the remaining nut filling.

• Grease a 30 x 25cm rectangular oven tray and place each filled roll on it, leaving a little space between them.

• When they are all in the tray, cut into slices with a sharp knife, then brush the surface with the remaining butter.

• Bake in the oven for 20 minutes. The surface should become golden and crispy.

• Remove from the oven and pour the sugar syrup over the rolls. Sprinkle with pistachios. Leave for 30 minutes in the tray before serving to absorb the syrup.

Walnut-Filled Pancakes

Katayef

During the month of Ramadan the shops are full of sweet goodies, *katayef* being one of the most popular. Throughout the month you will find plenty of these delicious pancakes in every patisserie, made fresh every few hours to keep up with the demand. This recipe makes 18 pancakes and enough filling for half to be stuffed with *Kashta* (milk curd) and half with walnuts.

MAKES 18 PANCAKES

100g plain flour
1 tsp instant dried yeast
1 tsp sugar
200ml lukewarm water
Oil, for frying

For the walnut filling
100g chopped walnuts
    resembling breadcrumbs
30g granulated sugar
1 tbsp *mazaher* (orange
    blossom water)
500ml aromatic Sugar Syrup
    (page 266)

For the curd filling
100g *kashta* (milk curd, page
    267) mixed with 30g
    whipped cream
10g ground pistachios
Candied orange petals, for
    decoration (optional, see
    also page 10)

Preparation time: 30 minutes
Cooking time: 30–40
    minutes

- Mix the flour, yeast, sugar and water and whisk until the mixture becomes like a batter and is lump-free. Cover and set aside at room temperature for approximately 1 hour to ferment and form bubbles.

- Meanwhile, prepare the walnut filling by mixing together the walnuts, sugar and *mazaher*.

- To make the pancakes, heat a heavy-bottomed pan or a griddle, drop 1 tablespoon of the batter onto the heated surface and spread out to about 10cm diameter with the back of a spoon. The pancakes are cooked when they stop bubbling on the surface and the bottom is very slightly brown. Note: cook on *one side only*.

- Remove the cooked pancakes and leave to cool on a piece of greaseproof paper.

- Place 1 teaspoon of the walnut filling in the centre of each pancake. Fold in half, then seal the edges by squeezing them together.

- Heat the oil in a frying pan and lightly fry the filled pancakes on both sides. Remove from the pan and drop them in a bowl of syrup. Allow 2 minutes before transferring to a serving plate.

- For the curd filling, place 1–2 teaspoons curd on each pancake, stick down one end of it just halfway to form a cone shape, sprinkle the top end with pistachios and garnish with a few orange petals, if available.

- Unlike the walnut-filled pancakes, this version is not fried but eaten uncooked and served with syrup on the side.

- Serve both types of pancake freshly made with syrup.

Semolina and Yogurt Cake

Nammoura

As young children, this was one of the street foods we could afford to buy with the little pocket money we had. We waited patiently after school for the street seller to turn up with his trolley. It was even better in the village, where the seller came with a donkey to carry his goods.

SERVES 6–8

150g unsalted butter
160g sugar
350g semolina
2 tsp baking powder
250g natural yogurt
1 tbsp tahini, for greasing
15–20 almonds, depending on the size of slices.
300ml cold Aromatic Sugar Syrup (page 266)

Preparation time: 15 minutes
Baking time: 45 minutes

• Preheat the oven to 180°C/350°F/gas mark 4.

• Cream the butter with the sugar.

• Add the semolina and the baking powder and mix to combine well.

• Add the yogurt and mix until smooth.

• Grease a baking tray measuring approximately 22 x 32cm with the tahini and spread the mixture evenly and smoothly over the base. Score the surface with a knife into squares and place an almond on each one.

• Bake in the preheated oven for 45 minutes.

• While still in the baking tray, cut into pieces along the scored lines and pour the cold syrup over the top. Allow the syrup to soak in while the cake is cooling, then transfer the squares to a serving plate.

Cook's tip
• It is always better to pour cold syrup onto hot cakes to avoid them becoming soggy. *Nammoura* is quite dense with syrup.

Semolina Cookies with Dates or Nuts

Maamool

Semolina is often used in Lebanese sweets and desserts. *Maamool* are little semolina cookies, filled either with dates or chopped nuts that melt in the mouth. A festive dish, they are always offered to guests around Easter time. They are time-consuming to make but well worth it and they keep well.

MAKES 24

For the pastry
250g semolina
150g plain flour
2 tsp dried yeast
200g melted unsalted butter
3 tbsp rose water (*maward*)
2 tbsp orange blossom water (*mazaher*)
50ml water, or just enough to hold the pastry

For the nut filling
200g walnuts or pistachios, chopped to resemble breadcrumbs
50g caster sugar
1/2 tbsp *mazaher*
1/2 tbsp *maward*
Icing sugar, for dusting

For the date filling
150g minced dates
30g melted, unsalted butter

Preparation time: 1 hour–1 hour, 30 minutes
Baking time: 30–35 minutes

• To make the pastry, mix together the semolina, flour and yeast, then pour in the melted butter to absorb into the dry ingredients. Add the *maward*, *mazaher* and water; mix well to form a smooth dough. Cover and leave for 6–10 hours at room temperature until the dough absorbs all the liquids.

• Preheat the oven to 190°C/375°F/gas mark 5. Line a baking tray with baking parchment.

• To make the nut filling, mix together the nuts, caster sugar, *mazaher* and *maward*.

• For the date filling, combine the minced dates with the melted butter.

• Knead the dough a few times to loosen it, then divide into small pieces and roll eack one into a golf-ball size. Flatten in the palms of your hands and spoon a teaspoon of nut or date filling into the centre. Make the nut-filled biscuits into a round shape; the date-filled ones are pressed to a flat shape (see photo).

• Seal and place on greaseproof paper, being sure to leave enough space between each one.

• We normally use a special mould for *maamool*. You may be able to buy the moulds online or from Middle Eastern shops, but if they are not available, just make a pattern on the tops of the cookies using the back of a fork. This is to hold the icing sugar and creates a pretty pattern.

• Bake for 30–35 minutes until the surface is very slightly browned.

- After removing from the oven, thickly dust the nut-filled *maamool* with icing sugar while they are hot. (The date-filled biscuits are sweet enough, so they don't need added sugar.)

- *Maamool* will keep in an airtight container for 2 to 3 weeks.

- Serve with tea or coffee.

Northern Rice Pudding with Cheese

Halawet el Rouz

This is not the usual rice pudding; it's not even known to many Lebanese. A speciality of the North, it's rare to find it in patisseries. I was given this very special recipe by a chef in one of the northern patisseries, although I was prepared to beg for it!

SERVES 4

80g pudding rice
600ml whole milk
60g icing sugar
1 tbsp *mazaher* (orange
  flower water)
1 tbsp *maward* (rose water)
1 x 220g ball of mozzarella,
  grated
½ tsp ground *miskeh*
  (mastic), if available (see
  also page 10–12)

For the topping
200g *kashta* (milk curd,
  page 267)
A little candied orange petals
  (optional, see also page 10)
1 tbsp crushed pistachios

Preparation time: 10 minutes
Cooking time: 1 hour

• Cook the rice in boiling water for 10 minutes, drain and add to the milk. Gently cook for about 40 minutes until the rice is very mushy.

• Purée the rice using a hand blender, then return the pan to the heat, add the icing sugar and stir for a few minutes. Add the *mazaher, maward*, mozzarella and *miskeh*. Continue to heat, stirring, for another minute or two.

• Turn out onto a flat serving dish or small individual dishes and leave to cool.

• When cold, spoon over the *kashta*, top with a few orange petals and sprinkle pistachios over the top. Cover with clingfilm and refrigerate for up to 2 days.

• Serve cold with a little Aromatic Sugar Syrup (page 266) on the side, if liked.

Cook's tips

• Candied orange petals are made like a jam, in heavy syrup, but never eaten as jam. They are only served with certain sweets.

• If you make this dessert, do not be tempted to use ground rice for an easier option. It is really not the same and not nearly as good.

Lebanese Nights

Layali Libnan

This simple dish is bursting with various aromatic flavours. As I mentioned earlier, we rarely have desserts after a meal; something like this is prepared and kept in the fridge for up to 2 days to have when you feel like something sweet or have guests.

SERVES 4

600ml whole milk
60g semolina
60g sugar
30g crushed pistachios
1 tbsp *mazaher* (orange
  blossom water)
1 tbsp *maward* (rose water)
1/2 tsp ground *miskeh*
  (mastic) (optional, see
  pages 10–12)
120g *kashta* (milk curd, page
  266)
100g whipped cream
100ml Aromatic Sugar Syrup
  (page 266)
25g candied orange blossom
  (optional)

Preparation time: 10 minutes
Cooking time: 25 minutes

• Combine the milk, semolina and sugar in a pan and stir until there are no lumps.

• Start heating the mixture, stirring all the time, until it begins to bubble.

• Turn the heat to low and cook for 20 minutes, stirring occasionally, until it becomes thick and fluffy.

• Add 10g of the pistachios, the *mazaher*, *maward* and *miskeh* (if using). Stir for 1 minute and remove from the heat. Turn out onto a serving dish and leave to cool at room temperature.

• Mix the *kashta* with the whipped cream. When the semolina is cool, spread it over the top and sprinkle with the remaining pistachios and a handful of candied orange blossom, if using.

• Keep in the fridge and serve cold with aromatic syrup.

Cook's tip
• Some people like to serve this dish with sliced bananas or strawberries.

Glazed Aniseed Shells

Macaroon

Macaroons are so easy to make that we were allowed to have fun making them as young kids (Mum did the frying). This is an old, traditional recipe but it's still very popular and we usually have lots of macaroons in the house to serve like biscuits. If you prefer, you can halve each of the ingredients to make less.

SERVES 10 PLUS

2 tbsp whole aniseeds
350ml water
400g plain flour
380g semolina
1 tsp baking powder or 2 tsp
  instant yeast
2 tsp sugar
2 tsp ground aniseeds
200ml olive oil
Oil, for deep-frying
500ml Aromatic Sugar Syrup
  (page 266)

Preparation time: 40 minutes
Cooking time: 30–35
  minutes

• Boil, then simmer whole aniseeds in the water for 10 minutes. Remove from the heat to cool down.

• Mix together the flour, semolina, baking powder or yeast, sugar and ground aniseeds.

• Add the olive oil and rub together with the dry ingredients until the mixture resembles a crumble.

• Strain the water from the aniseeds, which should be quite strong in flavour, and add it a little at a time to the dry ingredients, stirring until you have a smooth dough. Leave to rest for 1 hour. The aniseed water should be reduced to about 250ml.

• Take a small piece of dough, roll it into a small ball, then flatten in a colander to create a pattern on the macaroons. As you flatten it towards you it should curl; if it doesn't, roll with your hands to resemble a shell.

• Heat the oil and deep-fry the macaroons until they become golden brown. Remove from the heat and drop them into the sugar syrup.

• When you have finished frying and all the macaroons are in the syrup, leave for 5 minutes to absorb the syrup. The shells will keep for a week stored in an airtight container.

• Serve cold.

Almond Crescents

Lawzeyeh

Almond crescents are to be found in any patisserie in Lebanon. A delicious almond shortbread, they are very easy to make. Homemade *lawzeyeh* is always better than the bought kind.

MAKES UP TO 36, DEPENDING ON SIZE OF CUTTER

150g unsalted butter
35g caster sugar
180g plain white flour, plus extra for rolling out
100g chopped almonds (resembling breadcrumbs)
1–2 tsp almond essence
Icing sugar, for coating

Preparation time: 30 minutes, plus chilling the dough
Cooking time: 15 minutes

- Cream the butter to soften and then mix with the sugar.

- Sift the flour into the butter and sugar and combine well.

- Add the almonds and almond essence and keep mixing to combine all the ingredients.

- Wrap the dough in clingfilm (plastic wrap) and leave it in the fridge for at least half an hour.

- Preheat the oven to 180°C/350°F/gas mark 4.

- Roll the dough out onto a floured surface to about 1cm thick and cut it into crescent shapes using a cutter.

- Line a baking tray with a sheet of greaseproof paper, then place all the crescents on the paper, allowing space between them to spread. Bake in the preheated oven for 15 minutes.

- Allow to cool before removing from the baking tray and coating the biscuits with sifted icing sugar.

Cook's tip
- The cresents will keep for several weeks in an airtight container. They also freeze well for up to 8 weeks.

Quince Jam

Mraba Safarjal

Walking around the village in the autumn, the time when everyone is busy making jams and preparing for winter, you can smell the very distinctive aroma of the quince. It is made into a spreadable paste or served as slices of thick syrup to eat as a sweet treat.

MAKES ABOUT 4KG

For the spreadable jam
2kg quince, peeled and
  cored
2kg sugar
1 tbsp lemon juice
300ml water

Preparation time: 25 minutes
Cooking time: 1 hour, 25
  minutes

For the slices
1½kg quince, peeled and
  cored
1½kg sugar
Water, to cover the sugar
1 tbsp lemon juice

Preparation time: 20 minutes
Cooking time: 1 hour

• For the jam, prepare the jars by making sure they are thoroughly clean and dried. Any slight moisture in the jars will cause the jam to turn mouldy.

• Cut the quince into small pieces and place all the ingredients in a pan. Place on the hob and start cooking when all the ingredients are mixed together.

• When the mixture begins to bubble, turn the heat down and leave it to cook gently, stirring frequently.

• When the jam begins to thicken and becomes red in colour, test a little on a cold plate to make sure it's set. (My advice is to invest in a jam thermometer, so you know when the jam is ready – just over 100°C.)

• Using a ladle, transfer to the jars and screw the lids on firmly when cooled.

Cook's tip
• This is delicious served with cheese, although it's not the Lebanese way. Unopened jars will keep for up to 1 year.

For the slices.

• After peeling and coring the quince, keep them as whole slices and set aside for an hour to turn brown. This helps to give the red finished colour. I wasn't convinced about this initially, but it works!

• Put the remaining ingredients in a pan and begin cooking. When the sugar has dissolved, continue cooking on low heat for about 10 minutes. Add the quince slices.

• With this recipe, you don't need to stir as frequently as with the spreadable jam but only occasionally. This is to keep the slices whole while cooking in their own syrup, and less likely to stick to the bottom of the pan.

• You will know when the slices are ready as they turn a lovely rich red colour.

Fig Jam
Mraba Teen

Towards the end of the autumn season, figs become sweet and syrupy, leading to another ritualistic jam making. The Lebanese are not big on desserts after a meal, but often enjoy one or two mouthfuls of something sweet. Both quince and fig jam are often placed on the table after a meal for this purpose.

MAKES 1¹/₂KG

1kg figs
400g sugar
Juice of ¹/₂ lemon
¹/₂ tsp ground *miskeh*
   (mastic) (optional but
   recommended; see also
   pages 10–12)

Preparation time: 10 minutes
Cooking time: 1 hour, 25
   minutes

• Remove the stalks from the top of the figs, break them into halves with your fingers and place in a saucepan.

• Add the sugar and lemon juice. (Less sugar is required in this recipe because figs are naturally very sweet.)

• Place the pan on the hob and stir the mixture until it begins to boil, then turn the heat to low and simmer for about 1 hour.

• When the bubbles have reduced, the jam is a golden colour and has thickened, remove from the heat and add the ground *miskeh*, if using, and stir well.

• Transfer to clean, dry jars (see also page 240) and screw the lids on firmly when cooled.

Cook's tip
• *Miskeh* is usually used in milk desserts, so it's an exception to add it to fig jam – but as it compliments the taste of figs so well, it's highly recommended here.

Almond, Walnut and Sugar Roll

Mwaraka

This is a speciality of Furn el Sabaya in Lebanon ('young ladies bakery'), which I was privileged to visit and where I was taught to make this delicious pastry by the sisters who run this modest but very unique bakery. I also loved the idea of something sweet and tasty without a fatty pastry.

SERVES 4

150g plain flour, plus extra for rolling out
1 tsp instant dried yeast
Pinch of salt
75ml water
15g melted, unsalted butter
30g chopped walnuts
30g chopped whole almonds (skin on)
30g sugar
1/2 tbsp *mazaher* (orange blossom water)
1/2 tbsp *maward* (rose water)

Preparation time: 20 minutes, plus dough rising time
Baking time: 35 minutes

• Make the dough by mixing together the flour, yeast and salt. Add the water and knead for a few minutes. Cover the bowl and allow the dough to rise somewhere warm; this may take 1 hour or more to double in size.

• Preheat the oven to 220°C/425°F/gas mark 7.

• After the dough has risen, roll it out onto a floured surface as thinly as possible. Fold over into 4 layers and roll it again. Repeat two more times, then roll into a thin circle. Trim any uneven edges with a knife.

• Brush the edges of the dough with melted butter. Mix the nuts with sugar, *mazaher* and *maward*, then spread all over the dough except for the buttered edges.

• Make hole in the middle and begin to roll it outwards, one side at a time until you get to the buttered edge and seal.

• Hold the roll at one end and bring to the middle, so you have the twisted shape shown in the photos.

• Place on a baking tray, brush the surface with a little more butter and bake in the preheated oven for 35 minutes.

• Serve warm or cold.

Cook's tip
• It's important to fold the rolled dough a few times because this helps to make it flaky when baked.

Lebanese Bread Pudding
Aysh El-Saraya

This is a homemade pudding; it's never sold in shops. It is an extremely sweet Lebanese version of bread pudding but serving it with *kashta* (milk curd) tends to cut through the sweetness. I love the combination of flavours in this dish – just writing about it makes me want to eat it!

SERVES 6

1 small loaf white bread,
  kept for 1–2 days before
  using
250ml water
400g white sugar
1 tsp lemon juice
2 tbsp *mazaher* (orange
  blossom water)
Kashta (milk curd, page 267)
50g roughly ground pistachio
  nuts

Preparation time: 15 minutes
Cooking time: 20 minutes

• Prepare the bread by cutting off all the crusts then break it into small pieces and place in a serving dish.

• Make the syrup by adding the water, sugar and lemon juice to a saucepan and leave to boil for about 15 minutes to form a syrupy texture. Remove from the heat.

• Transfer half the syrup to another saucepan and boil until it turns a light brown colour, then stir in with the rest of the syrup. Now you have a dark caramelized syrup.

• Add the *mazaher* to the syrup and then pour over the bread and leave to cool. When cold, make sure the syrup and bread are well combined and squeeze into a firm, round shape; wrap in clingfilm then store it in the fridge for an hour or two.

• Spread *kashta* over the top and sprinkle with pistachios to serve.

• You can make this recipe in individual portions if you prefer.

Cook's tip
• This dessert gets better with time. You can still serve it after 3–4 days if kept in the fridge.

Dry Fruit Salad

Khashaf

This very traditional fruit salad is packed with a delectable combination of flavours, a mixture of different fruits together with nuts, rose water and orange blossom water. Don't worry if you have any leftovers because it will keep in the fridge for at least a week.

SERVES 4–6

100g dried figs
100g dried prunes, pitted
100g dried apricots, pitted, plus 300g for the coulis
100g sultanas
100g raw almonds
30g pine nuts
2 pieces of cinnamon bark, about 5cm each
300ml freshly squeezed orange juice
2 tbsp orange blossom water (*mazaher*)
2 tbsp rose water (*maward*)
2 tbsp crushed pistachios, for garnishing

Preparation time: 10–15 minutes, plus soaking time

• Slice the figs, prunes and 100g of the apricots into quarters, or smaller if preferred.

• Mix the chopped fruit with the sultanas, almonds, pine nuts, cinnamon bark, orange juice, *mazaher* and *maward*. Cover and leave to soak for at least 12 hours at room temperature.

• At the same time, soak the remaining apricots for the coulis in 400ml of water for the same length of time as the fruit mixture.

• Press the apricots through a sieve to achieve the consistency of a purée.

• Serve the fruit salad in small dishes, with the apricot coulis spooned on top.

• Garnish with crushed pistachios.

Cook's tip
• This dish can be served with natural yogurt or add a spoonful to your breakfast cereal, although the Lebanese don't normally have cereal. It has been introduced in Lebanese supermarkets in the last 10 years but hasn't caught on with everyone just yet.

Date Slices

Tamreyeh

Impress your friends when they turn up for a coffee with something very different. These delicious slices are the perfect partner for coffee. I've never bought *tamreyeh* from a patisserie because it's simple enough to make as well as being tastier. And it doesn't require any baking.

MAKES ABOUT 20 SLICES

500g block of pitted dates or any other moist dates
60g melted, unsalted butter
80g Rich Tea biscuits
100g broken walnuts
40g unsweetened, desiccated coconut

Preparation time: 15 minutes

• Blitz the date block in a food processor. Add the melted butter and mince the dates until they form a paste.

• Mix the processed dates with the biscuits and walnuts.

• On a smooth surface, roll the date mixture into a sausage shape, then roll on a plate of coconut to coat all over.

• Wrap clingfilm (plastic wrap) round the sausage and chill in the fridge for a couple of hours, which makes it easier to slice.

• Take the date roll out of the fridge, remove the clingfilm and cut into 1cm-thick, round slices.

• Delicious served with coffee.

Cook's tip
• Store the slices in an airtight container in the fridge, where they can be kept for 2 weeks, because they may stick together at room temperature.

Saida Shortbread with Pistachios

Sanyoura

Sanyoura have originated from the Southern city of Sidon (Saida). In Saida there are more patisseries than any other food shops. *Sanyoura* is what people are expected to take home from Saida. Mostly plain, it is sometimes filled with crushed pistachios. Here, I added the nuts to the pastry instead, which makes it both easier and tastier.

MAKES 15–20 BISCUITS, DEPENDING ON SIZE

125g icing sugar
250g plain flour
170g butter, softened at room temperature
60g crushed pistachios, reserving 15–20 whole ones for topping
1 tbsp *mazaher* (orange blossom water, optional)

Preparation time: 30 minutes
Baking time: 20–25 minutes

• Mix the icing sugar with the flour.

• Rub in the softened butter to form a ball of pastry and then add the nuts and combine with the pastry. Add the *mazaher*, if using, and allow it to rest for 15–30 minutes.

• Preheat the oven to 180°C/350°F/gas mark 4.

• Roll out the pastry dough out onto a sheet of greaseproof paper, without flouring, as this makes it easier to remove the *sanyoura* and transfer to a baking tray. It should be about 1cm thick.

• Use a knife to cut the dough into diamond shapes, then place a whole pistachio in the centre of each one.

• Arrange the *sanyoura* on a baking tray, preferably on a greaseproof layer, leaving a little space between the shortbreads to allow for spreading.

• Bake in the preheated oven for 20–25 minutes.

• When the *sanyoura* are cooled, store in an airtight biscuit tin for up to 2 weeks.

Spiced Rice Dessert
Meghli

For centuries people have followed the tradition of making *meghli* when a new baby is born. The family offer *meghli* to well-wishers who come to see the child for six weeks after the birth. All friends and relatives must visit the new parents, otherwise it may cause offence. This spicy dessert is topped extravagantly with nuts. Some people express either their wealth or generosity by the quantity of nuts they include.

SERVES 6

150g ground rice
150g sugar
15g ground cinnamon
4g ground aniseeds
3g ground caraway seeds
$\frac{1}{2}$ tsp ground ginger
1ltr cold water

For the topping
A handful of nuts: walnuts,
 almonds, pistachios and
 pine nuts
3–4 tbsp desiccated coconut

Preparation time: 5–10
 minutes, plus soaking the
 nuts
Cooking time: 1 hour

• Soak whatever nuts you decide to use for the topping in cold water for a couple of hours. This will make them plump up and taste like fresh nuts.

• Combine the ground rice, sugar and all the spices in a saucepan. Add the water and stir to dissolve, making sure there are no lumps.

• Begin cooking, over a medium heat, stirring all the time to avoid the rice turning lumpy, until it starts to bubble.

• Turn the heat to low and cook the rice slowly for about an hour until the rice looks smooth and light brown in colour.

• Divide the *meghli* into serving portions, allow to cool, then place in the fridge for 1–2 hours to chill and set.

• Decorate just before serving by sprinkling first the coconut, then the nuts over the top.

• Always serve cold.

Cook's tip
• *Meghli* makes a lovely dessert at any time if you happen to like cinnamon. You can freeze it for up to 2 months after cooking. Allow to defrost overnight in the fridge, then gently heat and simmer for 5 minutes before dividing into individual portions as above.

CHAPTER 8
Basic Recipes
Aklaat Asasiyeh

In this chapter are the basic recipes that you will be using for reference, when you start anyway. They are very simple and you will get to know them by heart before too long. All these recipes are an important part of Lebanese cooking and are used repeatedly.

It is important to keep a good stock of the mixed spices recipe (page 258), as you will need it fairly often. Once you've made this aromatic blend of nine spices, you'll never want to be without it!

The pickles are commonly used and therefore good to have on standby. Pickled aubergines are great to have as starters when you have nothing prepared; we have them all the time.

Here, you will also find traditional salad dressings and sauces, rice or *burghul* (bulgur wheat) as an alternative to rice, yogurt and yogurt cream cheese, plus how to make curd and the aromatic syrup needed for many sweet dishes.

Lebanese Mixed Spices

Bharat

This mix, usually made with seven spices, is commonly used in Lebanon. It can be difficult to get hold of elsewhere if you don't live near a Middle Eastern grocer. I visited my local spice shop in the village to ask what spices are used in the mix and to my surprise they gave me the recipe – containing *nine* wonderful spices instead of the seven I expected. Used in many dishes, I truly believe this recipe is a treasure in any store cupboard.

MAKES 185G

10g bay leaves
15g dried ginger (if not available, use ground ginger)
40g cinnamon sticks
15g whole nutmeg
15g cloves
50g pimento (allspice)
20g black peppercorns
10g white peppercorns
10g cardamom

Preparation time: 10 minutes

• Simply place all the whole spices in an electric grinder and grind for few minutes until you have a fine powder.

• Transfer to a sealed jar and it will last for at least 6 months.

• Use mixed spices in various recipes. They work particularly well with rice.

Cook's tip
• This recipe makes a great gift to share. I'm so pleased with it, I now make a large batch to give to my children and friends.

Yogurt Culture

Tarweeb Laban

If you make Lebanese food often, you must have a go at making your own yogurt because it has many uses in our cuisine. When you make a large pot of yogurt, it tends to be used up quickly but will keep in the fridge for up to two weeks; in fact, it is better to use mature yogurt for cooking. Apart from the convenience and lower cost, it tastes better than commercial brands.

MAKES 2 LITRES

2ltr full-fat or semi-skimmed milk
1 small carton of natural yogurt (150g)

Cooking time: 15 minutes

- Bring the milk to a boil over a medium heat, giving it a stir every few minutes to prevent it from sticking to the bottom of the pan. Transfer to a mixing bowl.

- Allow to cool and reach body temperature. I use the old, unsophisticated method, which is to dip my (very clean) little finger in the milk and count to 10! You should just be starting to feel the heat when you get to it.

- Cream the yogurt in the pot to avoid any lumps and then stir it into the milk, making sure it has dissolved.

- Cover the bowl and store in a reasonably warm place, such as an airing cupboard. In a normal room temperature, put a towel or a small blanket round the pot for extra warmth.

- Leave the mixture in the same place, undisturbed, for at least 6 hours to set. Disturbing the milk during the incubating process may prevent it from setting and turning into yogurt.

- Store in the fridge in an airtight container.

Yogurt Cream Cheese

Labneh

You'll find *labneh* in every fridge in Lebanon. It resembles cream cheese, except that it's made from plain yogurt, drained and concentrated. *Labneh* is always served with breakfast, used with other ingredients to make dips (see tip below) or for spreading on bread.

MAKES ABOUT 350G

1 ltr plain yogurt
$^1/_2$ tsp salt to dissolve in the
yogurt

You will also need a muslin
bag or cloth

Preparation time: A few
minutes, plus 5–6 hours
straining the yogurt

• Place a muslin bag or cloth over a sieve and pour the yogurt into it with $^1/_2$ teaspoon salt. Either leave it in the sieve or tie the bag onto a tap, and allow to drain.

• Leave the yogurt to drain for about 5 hours or overnight to a smooth and light cream-cheese consistency.

• Remove from the bag and keep in the fridge in an airtight container for up to 1 week.

• Drizzle with olive oil (optional) and serve with bread or toasted pitta bread, if served as a dip.

Cook's tip
• Try mixing a crushed clove of garlic into the *labneh*, sprinkling with a little dried mint and drizzling with a little olive oil. This makes a very delicious dip.

Lebanese Rice with Vermicelli

Rouz Be Shayriyeh

Most Lebanese don't expect to have rice without vermicelli. Once you've prepared it in this way, you'll never cook rice without it. It's so tasty that sometimes we just eat it dressed with plain yogurt.

SERVES 4

50ml cooking oil
70g vermicelli pasta,
　crumbled into 2–3cm
　pieces
250g rice, soaked for 30
　minutes–1 hour
1/2 tsp salt

Preparation time: 5 minutes
Cooking time: 20–25
　minutes

• Heat the oil, add the crumbled vermicelli and keep turning until it becomes golden brown. Keep a close eye on it because it turns brown very quickly. Drain off the excess oil.

• Add to the vermicelli in the pan the rice, salt and just enough water to top the rice by 1cm.

• Allow to boil until most of the moisture has evaporated, then turn the heat to low, cover and slowly simmer for 20 minutes.

• Turn only once with a wooden spoon while cooking, so the rice doesn't become sticky.

• Serve with stews.

Cook's tip

• To avoid the rice becoming sticky, never be generous with water. You are much safer adding a little water later if you think the rice isn't cooked enough. Although in some cultures people prefer the rice to be sticky, in Lebanon if the rice turns sticky, it is thrown away. This is why for an authentic Lebanese dish, it's important to add water as instructed in the recipes.

Tahini Sauce

Tarator

This creamy sauce is most commonly used whenever fish is served. It is also used as a salad dressing and sometimes for cooking and is delicious served with roasted vegetables. For Lebanese recipes always use the light-coloured version and not the whole dark tahini.

MAKES 250ML

100g tahini
2 tbsp lemon juice
1 clove garlic, crushed
1/2 tsp salt
About 100ml cold water

Preparation time: 5 minutes

- Combine the tahini and lemon juice with a spoon until the mixture becomes thick and fluffy.

- Blend in the garlic and salt.

- Start adding cold water a little at a time, making sure there are no lumps before you add more water. Keep adding and blending more water until the sauce is creamy with no lumps.

- Serve with roasted vegetables or as salad dressing.

Aromatic Sugar Syrup

Kator

The majority of Middle Eastern sweets are very syrupy and extremely sweet. The aroma is usually due to the addition of *mazaher* (orange blossom water).

MAKES 400ML

400g sugar
200ml water
A little squeeze of lemon
1 tbsp *mazaher* (orange blossom water)

Cooking time: 20 minutes

- Combine the sugar, water and lemon juice and start heating it while stirring to dissolve the sugar. Allow to boil on a low heat for 10 minutes.

- Spoon a little syrup onto a cold plate and check that it becomes thick and sticky when it cools.

- Remove from the heat and stir in the *mazaher*.

Cook's tip
- I make 1 litre of syrup to store in a jar in the fridge. It keeps for several weeks. It's worth doing this if it is used frequently.

Milk Curd

Kashta

Kashta resembles ricotta cheese. It is usually used in sweet dishes and often served on its own just with honey drizzled over and a few pine nuts sprinkled on top.

MAKES 500G

2ltr full-fat milk
Juice of 1 lemon

Cooking time: 15–20 minutes

- Boil the milk on a medium to low heat, stirring it occasionally to prevent it from sticking to the bottom of the pan.

- When the milk boils and begins to rise, add the lemon juice and soon afterwards you will notice the milk beginning to separate.

- As the curd thickens on the surface and you can see the thin whey forming underneath, start scooping out the curd with a slotted spoon and transfer it to a sieve to drain. Keep boiling until all the curd is scooped out.

- Allow the curd to cool and keep it in the fridge until required for up to 3 days.

- Serve with sweet dishes and fruit salad.

Cook's tip
- Often people mix the curd with whipped cream so it is easier to spread.

Traditional Lebanese Salad Dressing

Salsat Salata Libnaneyeh

This is the basic Lebanese salad dressing and it's the only one most people use. It's a simple dressing but it brings out the flavour in some mild dishes and beautifully complements the taste of Lebanese food.

1 tbsp lemon juice
1 tbsp olive oil
1 clove garlic, crushed
$\frac{1}{2}$ tsp salt

• Just mix all the ingredients together and add to the salad you choose to serve (when including raw garlic, it is better to use the dressing straight away rather than storing).

Preparation time: 5 minutes

Cooked Bulgur Wheat

Burghul Mfalfal

Country people store *burghul* for the whole year. It is used frequently, either served as a dish with various salads and sometimes as a substitute to rice, as many prefer it. *Burghul* comes in two variations, fine or coarse. Fine *burghul* is used in *tabouleh* and all the *kebbeh* dishes. The coarse variety is used for other cooked dishes, as indicated in the recipes.

SERVES 4

50ml oil
200g (1 large) onion, finely
   chopped
300g coarse *burghul* (bulgur
   wheat)
1 tsp salt

Preparation time: 5 minutes
Cooking time: 20–25
   minutes

• Heat the oil and fry the onion for 10 minutes to brown.

• Rinse the *burghul*, drain and add to the onion in the pan.

• Add the salt and enough water to just cover the surface of the *burghul*; continue to heat.

• When it starts to boil, turn the heat down to low, cover and leave to simmer for about 15 minutes until all the moisture has evaporated. Remember to give it one quick stir while simmering.

• Check it by tasting: if still a bit crunchy, just add a little more water and cook a little longer.

• Serve with Dried Bean Stew (page 154), Green Bean Stew (page 152) or a simple Cabbage Salad (page 62).

Cumin Rice

Rouz Bkammoun

Cumin rice is another alternative to plain cooked rice. It's quite unusual but adds a great taste to some dishes.

SERVES 4

50ml oil
1 medium onion, chopped
1 tsp ground cumin
1 tsp cumin seeds
250g basmati rice, soaked
  for 30 minutes
$^1/_2$ tsp salt

Preparation time: 5 minutes,
  plus soaking the rice
Cooking time: 25 minutes

• Heat the oil and fry the onion for 10 minutes to brown.

• Add the ground cumin and cumin seeds. Fry with the onion for a couple of minutes.

• Add the rice and salt, then add water to about 1cm above the rice.

• Leave to boil for a few minutes until the water on the surface has evaporated. Cover the pan and continue cooking the rice on a low heat until all the moisture has evaporated.

• Serve as an alternative to regular rice. It works especially well with tahini dishes.

Pickled White Turnips

Kabees Lift

Pickles in general are very popular in Lebanon. Growing up in Beirut, when we went to the funfair, it was a choice between pickles or candyfloss. Turnips are always top of the list. They are rarely used for cooking – most people only know turnips as pickled.

MAKES 1KG

1kg medium to small turnips
1 medium-sized raw beetroot
80g coarse sea salt
40g sugar
900ml warm water

Preparation time: 15 minutes

- Trim the ends off each turnip then cut them into quarters or slices.

- Peel and slice the beetroot (this gives the turnips a pink colour).

- Dilute the salt and sugar with the warm water.

- Stack the turnips in a jar, adding beetroot slices in between them.

- Pour the salted water over the turnips, making sure they are all covered.

- Screw the lid on tightly until they are ready to eat (after 1 month) and will keep for a further 4 months.

- Serve as a condiment with a variety of dishes such as *Mjadara* (page 204), *Foul Mdammas* (page 120), *Hummus* (page 30) and especially with falafel (page 144).

Pickled Stuffed Aubergines

Makdous Batingane

Pickled aubergines are to be found in almost every home. Usually served as a starter or side dish, or simply by themselves as a snack with bread, they keep for a long time and are always good to have in the house. They are filled with a delicious garlic, walnut and chilli stuffing and preserved in olive oil.

MAKES 12

12 baby aubergines
70g walnuts, chopped to a
  breadcrumb consistency
6 cloves garlic, chopped
1 tsp salt
2 red chillies, deseeded and
  chopped (optional)
1 tsp sea salt
Olive oil

Preparation time: 30
  minutes, plus 2 hours'
  drying
Cooking time: 5 minutes

• Blanche the aubergines in boiling water just to soften slightly but don't make them too soft.

• Place the aubergines on a tea towel, make a vertical slit in each one and allow to dry out for a few hours at room temperaure.

• To make a filling, mix the walnuts, garlic, 1 teaspoon salt and the chillies, if using. Fill each aubergine with a teaspoon of the filling and place in a sealed jar.

• Pour in enough olive oil to cover the aubergines, add the sea salt and screw the lid on tightly.

• Allow 2 weeks before they are ready to eat. Always store in the fridge and consume within 6 months, making sure the surface is covered in oil (top up, if necessary) to ensure they stay in good condition.

• ALWAYS serve with bread.

• When the aubergines are eaten, don't waste the oil but use it in salad dressings.

Index